Supernal Adventures

Exploring the New Normal of Multidimensional Living

Book Two: Supernal Living Series

by

Dana Taylor

Book One: Ever-Flowing Streams: Christ, Reiki, Reincarnation & Me

All rights reserved. No part of this book may be used or reproduced by any means, graphic, electronic, or mechanical, including photocopying, recording, taping of by any information storage retrieval system, or otherwise copied for public or private use--other than "fair use" as brief quotations embodied in critical articles and reviews-- without prior written permission of the publisher.

Supernal Living Publishing

SupernalFriends@yahoo.com

www.SupernalLiving.com

I0200246

Copyright © 2016 Dana Taylor. All Rights Reserved

ISBN-13 9780692668009 ISBN-10 0692668004

The author of this book does not dispense medical advice or prescribe the use of any technique as a form of treatment for physical, emotional, or medical problems without the advice of a physician, either directly or indirectly. The intent of the author is only to offer information of a general nature to help you in your quest for emotional and spiritual well-being. In the event you use any of the information in this book, which is your constitutional right, the author assumes no responsibility for your actions.

Dedication

To my Supernal Friends ~ Paula, Sue, and Helen.
You bring Light, Laughter, and Love to the world

Table of Contents

Prologue ~ Supernal Adventures Begin

"Hello, Sappho"
Oklahoma City, September 2005
Joanne's Akashic Record Reading

The door to the inner office closed behind me. *I'll never be able to tell my husband about this.* My legs felt wobbly as I took a seat in one of two finely appointed leather Queen Anne chairs. Joanne, the Akashic Records reader, sat in the other chair. A cozy little table created a small distance between us.

Her wide, beautiful wooden desk sat on the other side of the room. A lush Oriental carpet cushioned our feet for this spiritual trip to the realm of the Akash.

A long credenza rested against the wall behind her, laden with the mysterious tools of her trade--drums, metal and crystal bowls, rocks and glittering stones, feathery dream catchers. The air enveloped us with whiffs of various essential oils. Sandalwood and sage?

Joanne may have been a seer, but she looked very Midwestern. Her roundish face and figure reflected a meat-and-potatoes Oklahoma diet. The blond hair and pale coloring recalled the European gene pool of her ancestors.

Before the session began, she'd explained to Sue, Paula, and me what to expect. The Akashic Records, she said, also called the Book of Life in the Bible, keeps an accounting of all our incarnations. The guides and keepers of the records can be consulted through connection with an earthly Akashic Records reader. Only our individual records could be accessed. We couldn't ask questions about other people, except how they related to us. Certificates on the wall attested to her skills.

Sue had eagerly volunteered for the first reading, leaving Paula and me to squirm in the waiting room. Sue was the instigator of this adventure. Sue the fearless. Sue, with the warrior's heart. She'd thought it quite the lark to get an Akashic Records reading during her visit to Oklahoma City. Only $100 to tap into the wisdom of the ages. A bargain!

As I'd cooled my heels in the waiting room, the quote from P.T. Barnum echoed in my head, *There's a sucker born every minute.*

Now it was my turn in the hot seat. Joanne stood up and walked over to the credenza. She approached a large opaque white crystal bowl, picked up a wand, and began circling the rim of the bowl. A high pitched note began to hum, softly...louder, louder, LOUDER still. It turned into a siren, ringing the whole room with a vibration that surely would have set dogs to howling. I barely restrained covering my ears.

She lifted the wand and the sound slowly dissipated. As she returned to her seat and settled back into the leather she said, "They told me to do that."

Okey, dokey then.

My hands trembled slightly from pent up nerves as I clutched the page of my prepared questions. Coming up with pointed queries to ask of exalted, wise, unseen Guardians is not easy. You don't want to waste their time or be frivolous, right?

I sat silently waiting to take my cue from Joanne. She recited a prayer and her face shifted somehow. Her eyes stared off to an unseen horizon. It was a little spooky, but intriguing. She indicated she was ready for the first question.

I asked her about the most puzzling, continuous theme of my life. "Why do I have this never-ending, constant urge to write?"

She smiled slightly and said, "Hello, Sappho."

I vaguely recalled Sappho was some ancient Greek, associated with the arts. From there came questions and answers about relationships, life goals, direction for the near future. She told me I served as a teacher for my husband and my nephew. I would speak to large groups of people. I would show my church a paradigm shift. She encouraged me to go take care of my father.

Later, over drinks at a lakeside cantina, Sue, Paula, and I shared our experiences with Joanne. Sue had supposedly known Jesus in a previous life. Paula had Padre Pio as one of her guides. We had a high time teasing each other recalling our afternoon.

Akashic Record readings from the seer Joanne kicked off our Supernal Adventures.

Chapter One ~ Better Write That Down

It's been ten years since that fateful week. Sue, Paula, and I have been spiritual explorers, of sorts. Our understanding of how the universe works has shifted, expanded, and sometimes turned cartwheels. We've lived fairly normal, middle class American lives. Sue and Paula are sisters, often seeming like flip sides of the same coin. Sue is blond with ivory skin; Paula is brunette with an olive complexion. Sue is out going, funny and often boisterous. Paula is reserved and spent much of her life feeling shy. I am their soul sister, having known them for over four decades. Sue and I met in our Southern California high school drama department and became fast friends. We've commiserated through boyfriends, husbands, children, jobs, and family deaths. We're at the stage now of welcoming grandchildren into our lives.

A life changing event for all of us was the healing Paula experienced that week of September, 2005, in Oklahoma City. Though I was born and raised in California, I'd married an Oklahoma lawyer in 1976. We raised our family in Oklahoma City. Paula and Sue raised their families in California, yet we always kept in touch. Paula spent most of her adult life experiencing health challenges, accidents, and strange medical conditions. Finally in her forties, a fall led to a condition called RSD (Reflex Sympathetic Dystrophy) or CRP (Complex Regional Pain). RSD is an excruciatingly painful nervous system condition. Basically, the brain never stops the pain response from an injury.

It is a progressive disease that cripples and finally kills. Paula spent seven years riding the waves of RSD, sometimes better and then taking a turn for the worse. Unrelenting pain robbed all the joy from life. Increasing medications wore away her ability to think, read, or really engage in life. Two battery devices were implanted in her back with wires attached to her spinal cord in an attempt to cut the pain. Her mobility was affected and she often used a cane.

By the summer of 2005 she was sliding down the slope towards becoming a true invalid. She was part of a study group with top doctors from UCLA. Despite being on 28 medications and the battery implants, the doctors told her the disease was progressing. She needed to prepare for a life in a wheelchair.

Sue, along with Paula's husband, Wayne, were her primary support partners. Their positive attitudes often lifted her out of the doldrums, but her daily life was unquestionably limited and bleak.

Sue and I discussed Paula often. Sue ached for her sister, and she never gave up hope. Time and again she would say, "I don't know how or when, but I know that Paula is not going to have this disease forever. I know she is going to get well."

In the spring of 2005, I met Helen, an English-born Reiki therapist, practicing in Oklahoma City. My first appointment with her was a life changing experience for me, as chronicled in *Ever-Flowing Streams: Christ, Reiki, Reincarnation & Me*. Since the doctors had given up on helping Paula get better, Sue and I hatched the idea that Paula should come to Oklahoma City and receive Reiki treatments from Helen. What did she have to lose?

Until that point, Paula had been fairly closed to alternative medicine and conscientiously followed the instructions of her many doctors. Now the doctors were out of drugs and therapies. Grasping at straws, Paula agreed to travel to Oklahoma City for energy healing treatments. They were the last resort.

Excerpt

Here is an excerpt from *Ever-Flowing Streams* recalling that week:

In early September of 2005, as the first hints of fall scented the air, Paula and Sue landed at the Oklahoma City airport. I spotted Paula sitting in a blue plastic chair, leaning on her cane, looking wan. Sue was wrangling all their luggage from the baggage claim carousels alone.

They had scheduled several appointments to see Helen over the next few days. What the week would bring was anybody's guess, but we'd make the best of it, even disappointment.

The next day I drove them to Helen's modest office. She greeted my friends in her characteristically cheerful manner, exuding Mary Poppins charm. Sue later told me she felt instant love for Helen, as if she'd found a long-lost daughter.

Helen worked on Sue first, while I ran some errands, leaving the girls in the healer's capable hands. An hour later, I dropped by and found Sue in the waiting room while Paula lay on the table in the therapy area. Sue and I tiptoed out to get a limeade.

I'll never know the intimate details of that session. Helen keeps the strictest healer/patient confidence and Paula was under the influence of pain meds and exhaustion. She did report an immediate jolt to her left side, as if a flow of energy and blood suddenly released from a pent-up dam. She fell asleep through much of the treatment and required a long nap afterwards.

The next day Paula entered Helen's office feeling better, with a lessened degree of pain and clearer head after a night's sleep. Lying on the therapy table, she enjoyed the warmth and sense of peace exuding from Helen's hands.

Thinking back, Paula relates, "I knew I felt good and appreciated the relief from relentless pain. I thought it was temporary. I never expected the pain to be permanently gone."

During the session, Helen received some information from her guides and said, "I think you're going to be working with children in areas of healing. I'm being told to offer you a first level Reiki attunement. It's entirely up to you if you want to receive it. Think about it. I can do it at our next session."

That gave Paula pause. Was she actually to become a Reiki practitioner herself? Only last week she'd been half-heartedly going along with her sister's plans on this quirky trip and now was she supposed to jump into the Reiki boat with both feet? Leaving the session pain-free but tired, she returned to the hotel room for another nap and a chance to ponder receiving the Reiki attunement.

The sisters came to my house that night for dinner and we sat afterwards in my backyard and talked for hours. The evening resides in my memory as a magical moment, a precious milestone.

Humidity hugged our skin as we sat under two huge maple trees. Trickling water trilled merrily from my little pond waterfall. Fireflies winked and fluttered—a horde of Tinker Bell fairies in our midst. Even the mosquitoes appeared enchanted, allowing us to chatter without driving us indoors.

Paula was happier, healthier. Alert. Engaged. We discussed the events of the day. I related my experience receiving a Reiki attunement. I don't remember what else we talked about, but laughter filled the evening air and nobody seemed sick.

In the motel room that night the enormity of the day caught up with the sisters. Paula sat on one bed, casually scratching a mosquito bite on her left leg when reality struck her.

"Oh my gosh, Sue, I'm scratching my RSD leg. Look at all the bites! And look…it's normal. There's no pain and no flare up of my leg!"

Sue stared at her sister's leg, "Oh my God, you're right."

Experience had taught them that scratching her bum leg could soon be followed by a trip to the emergency room. The RSD could kick in with swelling and excruciating pain, requiring immediate medical attention.

They looked at each other in alarm, recalling a botched trip to Hawaii when one bite had sent Paula into a major flare up. Her leg had ballooned and forced her into a wheelchair for the rest of the stay. Now she had a dozen bites and barely noticed! Her leg was…normal. She could scratch. .. She could walk…She could sleep.

The sisters stared at each other in shocked silence and amazement. They knew something good had definitely happened.

The "incurable" disease was gone. (End of excerpt)

As the months unfolded, our wonder at Paula's healing grew. At first we feared it was merely a placebo effect, but the pain and symptoms did not return. Paula weaned herself off of her medications. Her doctors' reactions ranged from hostile to incredulous. She eventually ceased seeing them. She and Wayne began moving towards new possibilities for their life together.

During that period, I found myself spending more time in California than Oklahoma taking care of my father, whose health was deteriorating. Sue, Paula, and I began holding meditation and healing sessions together. We dubbed ourselves the Supernal Friends. "Supernal" means "heavenly" or from "on high."

Paula represented living proof that Reiki and other modalities of energy healing were real. Some might call her healing a "miracle," a piece of luck, a whim of God. We didn't see it that way. Her healing represented a mystery and opened new avenues of study. The reality of spiritual realms and somehow tapping into higher energy information seemed suddenly possible. Even for grandmothers from Southern California.

I kept notes and journals as the years unfolded. Our Supernal Sessions became an opportunity for unseen spiritual teachers to reach out to willing students. Our spiritual gifts became more evident. Paula had certainly suffered the most in her life; her spiritual gifts appear to be the greatest. The ability to hear messages, see angels, departed souls, even channel higher energy entities revealed itself over the course of time. Sue became increasingly clairaudient. She hears music, messages, and even poems. As for me, I get little movies in my mind, see symbols, and feel energy. I have a knack as a medical intuitive and energy healer. Our ability to transmit healing energy both near and far sharpened. We kept our Supernal Sessions strictly secret between ourselves for a long time. Being labeled as kooks and dismissed as dotty old women held no appeal.

But, times they are a changin'. Reiki is now utilized in hospitals across the country. Classes are taught in colleges, along with reflexology, kinesiology, shiatsu and beyond. The power of crystals and stones is explored in the Silicon Valley, medical research, and space programs. Teresa Caputo, the Long Island medium, demonstrated that a seemingly "ordinary" wife and mother can possess very extraordinary gifts. Mediumship schools are popping up across the country. In Christian circles, the International House of Prayer in Kansas City is leading the vanguard of spiritual exploration within the context of Christian faith. The Internet has exploded with spiritual communities. I created a Reiki Room in my home and before I knew it, my phone began ringing with requests for treatments.

Now feels like the right time to crack open the Supernal Friends' journals and let them be an inspiration for discussion of many topics that have come up along the way. This book is not to be held out as an authority on any particular subject. Instead, let it stir your curiosity, entice your spiritual nature, open your mind to...possibilities.

Chapter Two ~ Energy Healing

Supernal Journals ~ January 31, 2014

Sylvia (named changed) has a rare form of non-Hodgkins lymphoma and heart problems. She is open to all forms of spiritual and healing exploration. I've gotten the impression her physical challenges are rooted in her DNA and are partly family karmic in origin. If her DNA can be altered, the effect will ripple into her whole family.

Our session last evening was fairly amazing. I felt a difference in air temperature and density in some parts of the room, as if other people were standing around the table. The energy flowing through me was so intense at times, I was afraid I might fall down.

Sylvia sometimes seemed to fall asleep. When I was working with a helper over her pelvic area, she jerked awake. She'd had a vision of her bone and marrow. It seems repairs in her blood and body fluids must be made. Currently, the most obvious challenge is her enlarged spleen.

I also felt guided to make her a funky raw stone necklace and infuse it with healing energy.

Update ~ April 2015. Sylvia is doing well, despite many work and family challenges. She is very proactive about her health, regularly juicing and eating all organic. Her spleen reduced in size and doctors are not currently recommending surgery.

How Do You Work With Healing Energy?

Asking me to discuss how to work with healing energy is like asking an adult how they walk. No physically able person thinks about walking after the age of two. We just do it. Analyzing the process is cumbersome. *First I lift one leg from the hip, bend my knee, propel the leg forward, touch the heel of the foot down, then push off from the ball of the foot. Then I do the same thing with the other leg.*

How does a child learn to walk? One step at a time. Step, fall down, stand up, step. One step, two step...three. Fall down. Stand up. Over and over again until the whole body learns to balance, coordinate, walk, run...dance!

Developing the ability to conduct healing energy is very similar. Practice and dogged devotion. Reading books and going to seminars is fine, but no child learned to walk just by watching others do it. If you seriously want to be a healer, you have to spend quiet time learning to sense the energy. Getting in touch with Higher Intelligence. Tuning into quantum information fields.

Study the chakras. The Eastern system of the energetic highways of the human body is thousands of years old. The West is just beginning to catch on. Vibrational medicine is gaining validity as science is increasingly able to chart the magnetic fields in and around our physical bodies.

It Starts In Your Head

The Hindus paint a "third eye" in the middle of their forehead to denote their connection to spirit. Paintings of Jesus and the saints often depict a glowing halo over their crowns. These are artistic representations of the very real point of contact for divine energy and humans in the brain.

Western physicians have identified the spot as the pineal gland, a tiny pinecone-shaped organ deep in the center of the brain. Scientific studies reveal it is responsible for the release of melatonin, the sleeping hormone. Metaphysicians have long associated the pineal gland with psychic activity. The 17th century philosopher Rene Descartes named it "the seat of the soul."

Pineal stimulation appears to be key in running healing energy. The pineal can become calcified from fluoridated water, poor diet, and other pollutants. An Internet search reveals a variety of suggestions to improve pineal health, the simplest being 20 minutes a day of exposure to fresh air and sunshine. People interested in working with healing energy should take the health of their pineal gland into consideration. An overall improvement in health could be a welcome side effect. The pineal may be tiny, but it plays an important role in hormonal balance.

I guess it shouldn't come as a surprise that a side-effect of meditation and healing energy work is improved sleep. Since the pineal controls the production of the sleep hormone, it stands to reason that a healthy pineal will produce good sleep. Reiki treatments and the numerous attunements through the years have transformed me from a terrible insomniac to a fabulous sleeper. This has happened at the age when most women going through menopause begin losing their ability to sleep well. I still regard sleep as a daily miracle.

Start Small

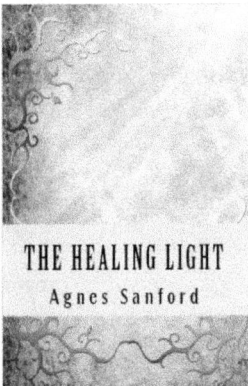

THE HEALING LIGHT
Agnes Sanford

Channeling healing energy is a very physical experience. The top of the head often feels enlarged and "buzzy." When I first began healing prayer, I used the model from Christian healer Agnes Sanford in *The Healing Light*. I pictured a beam of white light from the heavens flooding through the ceiling into my head, down my arms, and through my hands.

I practiced and practiced and practiced. I remember clearly sitting in church one day doing the visualization during a prayer and feeling the top of my head "expand" and "buzz."

Begin with small healing projects. One of my clients told me about channeling energy to her sick goldfish and seeing immediate results. Animals are wonderful receptors of healing energy. Success with them will build your confidence.

One of my most amazing healing experiences took place with my beloved cat, Buddy. Here is the post I wrote at my website, Supernal Living.

Buddy's Kitty Miracle ~ March 22, 2012

I really thought Buddy was a goner. My ten-year-old tuxedo cat walked in the house three nights ago and looked radically different. His walk wobbled and his coat looked oddly spiky. His eyes telegraphed pain.

"Buddy, what's wrong?" I asked. Of course, he didn't answer, but he didn't eat any dinner either, so I knew something was amiss. Stones came into my mind. Like humans, cats can develop painful stone blockages in their kidneys or bladders.

I immediately picked up the phone and alerted the Supernal Friends, "Pray for Buddy!"

The following afternoon I received a call from Helen. She said, "I'm afraid Buddy has stones in the urinary tract."

Helen worked several years in an emergency vet hospital and has experience with sick animals. She warned me that his condition was very painful. She told me I could tell if his bladder was obstructed by feeling for a hard ball near his belly. Worst case scenario, the bladder would burst and cause an excruciating death. Together we agreed that given his age and the expense of IV's and catheter treatment, my kindest solution was probably to put Buddy down.

Sitting in my backyard, with the sun shining and the birdies singing, I contemplated a sad trip in the morning to a vet. So, I did what a girl naturally does, I decided to get a haircut. If I was going to kill my cat, at least I would look good.

When I returned from the beauty shop, neatly trimmed, Buddy was lying on the warm concrete beside the pool. I went outside and petted him. He softly purred, but didn't have much energy to move. I poked around his belly and found a hard lump, somewhat smaller than a golf ball, just as Helen had predicted. Poor Buddy's bladder was completely blocked.

So, then I did the only thing I knew to do--I prayed. I laid my hands on Buddy's flanks, opened the energy centers in my head and hands, and prayed from the heart, "Please help my cat."

I allowed the spirit language I received long ago to flow, along with the healing energy and loving intention to bring Buddy relief. Sometimes prayer power simply kicks in and goes beyond human explanation. This was one of those moments. My prayer language expanded, chanting and flowing, as the buzz of the healing frequencies vibrated my hands. Both Buddy and I jolted a few times with the spurts of energy pouring through us. Sitting on the warm concrete, with the sky turning sunset colors, Buddy and I shared a heavenly moment. The experience lasted about ten minutes. The phrases subsided...the energy decreased....we came back to earth.

I patted him on the head and returned to the house. An hour later, I looked out the living room window and saw Buddy still lying where I'd left him. I did a double take--a river of fluid appeared to be flowing from his hind quarters. Had his bladder burst? Opening the screen door, I approached him with trepidation. His body was intact; he was alive and leaking urine like a Betsy Wetsy doll. Good grief! Who knew a cat could hold so much fluid? I massaged his belly, causing even more flow.

"Wow, Buddy. I think you are a kitty miracle." He then stood up and wobbled over to his water bowl and drank for the first time in two days.

That evening, he continued to be an incontinent cat. He clawed on the screen door to come into the house. "Buddy," I said. "I can't have you dripping cat pee all over my house. I'm sorry."

Sad-green cat eyes pleaded, "Let me in, mommy." I relented and opened the door. The carpets need to be cleaned anyway.

Being a gentleman, he walked directly to my bathroom and planted himself on the small rug, as if to say, "I won't mess up your house. You can wash this carpet." He stayed there all night long.

Another day has gone by. He is drinking water, lapping a little broth from his canned cat food and soaking up the rays by the pool. He's obviously more comfortable. I know he won't live forever; he's getting on in years. This crisis may hasten his demise. But, for now, he is my living testament that the power of Love is at our finger tips if we just learn how to channel it and allow it to flow through us.

Buddy lives on.

19

Update ~ April 2015. Buddy lived another year and never had another obstruction. He passed peacefully of old age beneath my hands on Thanksgiving day 2013.

Get Alone

In this day of ubiquitous entertainment and noise, solitude is a precious commodity. If you want to be an energy healer, create a quiet corner and carve out some "me" time, preferably not when you're overtired. Make it a priority. It may feel like you're "doing nothing," but praying and sending healing energy may be the most important part of your day.

Learn to play with the energy:

• Create an "energy ball" by cupping your hands a few inches apart and imagine sending white light into each palm. After a while you should feel the magnetic push against each hand.

• Sense the heat and pulse of the frequency in your head and down your arms. Turn off the lights. You may see your auric glow.

• Move your hands above your body a few inches and feel the warmth.

• Target a physical area--creaky knee, sore wrists, a small wound, some chronic annoyance--and pulse your hands over the area, visualizing healing energy radiating and soothing.

• Work with a willing pet, child, or partner on an area of concern. Administer daily healing treatments.

Use your intuition and see where it leads. If you invest the time, you will be amazed. You'll have small "a-ha" moments! A goldfish surges back to life, a cat's infection suddenly drains, a cut heals quickly, a toothache disappears. You'll wonder--*did that really happen?*

The "a-ha" moments add up to faith and confidence that healing energy is for real.

And that's when the real fun begins.

You're Not Alone

We talk about "working with the energy" as if it is a different sort of electricity, a laser than can be turned on and off. Simply an unseen force to be utilized. And that's true. But there's more.

There isn't just energy. There is intelligence. Perhaps I should say Intelligence--with a capital "I." It doesn't take long working quietly in healing energy, prayer, and meditation before you realize, you're definitely not alone.

This is where some people turn off the meditation music, turn on the lights, and forget the whole thing because it feels too weird. Old programming about demons and possession and fear-based theology rings too many bells. They get scared.

What was the first thing the angel said to Mother Mary? "Fear not!"

It's a natural reaction. Sensing multidimensional entities is part of the experience. In truth, energy healing is a partnership and exercise in co-creation with Spirit.

Who or what you are working with is certainly a Big Question. The answer may be simpler than you think: Who did you invite?

You can set your parameters of helpers through intention. Some people only want to work with Christ through the Holy Spirit. If that's where you're comfortable, clearly set out those requests as you begin your meditation.

Others want to work with Archangels, Ascended Masters, and Saints. So be it.

Indigenous healers work in their unique realms with their spirit guides and animals.

There even appears to be a host of extra-terrestrials getting into the act--Pleiadians and blue beings from Sirius, for a start. I know it sounds pure sci-fi, but check out the Internet. You'll see some very credible-sounding people sharing their experiences.

The point is, energy healing will get you in touch with other dimensions and the intelligent beings that travel there. You always have control of whether you want to deal with them or not. You're not possessed, you're in partnership.

In My Case

I began healing through Christian prayer groups. I feel comfortable inviting the Holy Spirit, the Christ Spirit, and angels. That's my orientation. There's also the concept of the Higher Self--the part of me that is on the other side of the veil. It seems I am often simply gaining information from myself at a higher level of awareness.

Everyday begins with about an hour of prayer, a cup of tea by my side. Tibetan singing bowls playing from YouTube set the mood. I begin with *The Lord's Prayer*, visualizing my chakra's from the crown down opening up.

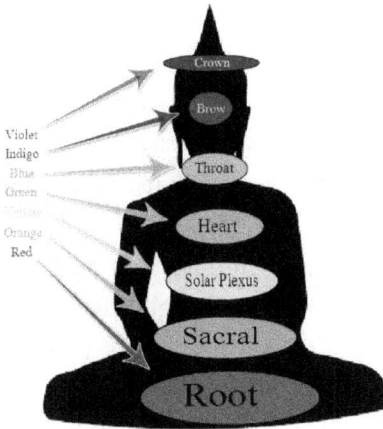

Violet
Indigo
Blue
Green
Yellow
Orange
Red

Crown
Brow
Throat
Heart
Solar Plexus
Sacral
Root

Our Father who art in heaven—white light above the head

Hallowed be thy name—purple light beaming into the forehead

Thy kingdom come—blue light to the throat

Thy will be done, On earth as it is in heaven—green light opens the heart

Give us this day our daily bread—yellow light feeds the stomach

Forgive us our debts, as we forgive our debtors—orange light below the belly button

And lead us not into temptation, but deliver us from evil—red light to the sexual centers

For thine is the kingdom and the power and the glory forever. Amen —run the energy into the earth down for grounding

I've created a comfortable, protected space and invite my "team" to join me and show who or what to pray for. Truthfully, I'm not sure who all is on the "team." I'm not that psychic. But I feel loved and connected. I suspect "team" members may change. There have been times I've sensed a large Blue Angel. Paula has seen such a being. (A helper from Sirius?) That presence is usually accompanied by coolness and a sense of increased air density.

Most days I feel the expanded head, warmth, buzzing energy and great peace. I begin to pray and send energy through visualization, often focusing on prayer requests. Images come. Surges of energy may jolt my whole body.

I ask where else to send energy. More images--the oceans, the Middle East, the White House. An underground mine. An unfamiliar city. Wherever. Once I was told to pray for Hillary Clinton. Later that day I learned she had been very sick and taken a serious fall. It's not usually so specific.

Random people pop up in my mind. I send energy. Often I soon hear from them "out-of-the blue." A few months ago, in my meditation time I recalled when my daughter had mononucleosis as a teenager. The doctor hadn't offered any medication, so I had researched herbal remedies. I put her on a course of Reishi mushroom tablets. Later that day she called and mentioned how worried she was about a girl she was sending overseas who had just been diagnosed with mononucleosis. Snap, the Reishi mushroom remedy popped back into my mind. "Funny" how I had just thought of it that morning.

Energy, information, and Higher Intelligence is all involved in this wonderful avenue of multidimensional living. Often the most intense healing sessions feel almost like a dream. The memories can fade quickly. Journaling during and after meditations is necessary to preserve the impressions, otherwise they scatter like the seeds of a dandelion, lost in the wind.

A Most Amazing Healing

In August of 2012 I converted an extra bedroom in my Southern California home into a Reiki Room, which turned into my Field of Dreams-- "build it and they will come."

I received a call from a woman named Joan. "Hi," she said. "I hear that you're an incredible healer and I would like to set an appointment."

Uh.... "incredible healer" felt greatly exaggerated. The dead had not been raised. The blind did not see. At best, it seemed I could boost a person's own healing abilities through energy healing.

We scheduled a session and I hoped that she wouldn't be disappointed.

Joan arrived right on time. A slim, attractive woman of Korean descent, but with a decidedly Southern California vibe. Her dark, casual clothes and long hair made her appear to be a college student, but in truth she was a 40ish corporate banker.

We hit it right off. She was wildly curious about Reiki, with a good dose of skepticism. I had no idea exactly why she wanted a treatment. At first glance, she appeared very fit.

She hopped onto the table, removed her shoes, laid back and watched me like a hawk. I began the New Age music and went through my routine of opening her chakras. A scan over her body revealed a very wide hot spot over her neck and shoulders. An image of crooked and crimped bones at the back of her neck appeared in my mind's eye.

I began working the area, pulling and drawing the energetic strands.

"Okay," she said. "I'm a believer."

As it turned out she was suffering residue neck and shoulder pain from a car accident experienced several months before. She was impressed when I zeroed in on the area. Also, she was sensitive to the energy and could feel it in various ways. After the session, I advised her to find a good massage therapist or chiropractor to work her neck and muscles into alignment, which she did.

A month later she scheduled another appointment. The first Reiki treatment seemed to get her in a better place in several ways and she wanted to keep up the momentum. September is the warmest month in Southern California. My house was not air conditioned. The Reiki Room was the hottest room in the house. I advised her that unless we did an early morning session, the room would probably be very uncomfortable.

"Heat doesn't bother me," she said. Being so skinny, I suppose it didn't, but I am not so impervious. Nevertheless, we scheduled an afternoon appointment time and I set up a couple of fans.

After she arrived, we chatted about her life. One fact that came out was a mysterious digestive disorder that struck her at about the age of 23. She suddenly became allergic to almost all food. Meat made her especially ill. Her skin broke out in sores. Her bowels seized and felt like stabbing knives. She couldn't eat dairy, wheat, or even vegetables that were cooked in a pot that had previously prepared meat. For a time she could only safely consume rice and tofu. She'd lived on vegetables and rice for fifteen years, out of necessity, not choice.

Joan has the spirit of a true foodie, delighting in exploring epicurean novelties. Alas, her body could not cooperate. However, she had learned to manage her diet, though it certainly put a damper on her social life. Eating out with friends in restaurants was nearly impossible unless she brought her own food. What fun is it to go out and watch everyone else eat while you scoop out your cold rice? Not very much. Her coworkers planned special foods for office parties just for Joan. Boring rice cakes or some such stuff. Joan had come to accept her limitations with good humor.

We started the session. Despite fans moving air, the room was hot, probably around 90 degrees or more. Joan lay quietly on the table, eyes closed. I worked around her body once. I stood at her head, feeling the top chakra wide open and flowing energy full throttle.

Coolness whispered around my legs. This was familiar and unmistakable. My Blue Angel had arrived. In other settings I always felt a kernel of doubt that the sense of coolness was merely imagination. That day was too hot and only getting hotter for any strand of cool air to suddenly be flitting in from a window.

Next an odd "shadow" appeared on the white wall. I saw a head, shoulders, and wings. Not really a shadow, more a light flash, like a repeating image from a flashlight bulb. Head, shoulders, wings moving up the wall, disappearing and beginning again. Head, shoulders, wings.

I stood at Joan's head still channeling energy and observing these strange happenings. Cold air. On a broiling hot day. I looked around for what could be a source of the odd shadow. Nothing unusual. Yet, there they were -- head, shoulders, wings.

I stepped to her side and began to sense guidance on where and how to move my hands. As I lifted my hands over Joan's abdomen, a stab of pain grabbed me, literally in the butt. I'd experienced client ghost pain before, but this was very strong.

I said, "You weren't kidding when you said you have intestinal pain. This hurts."

Joan opened her eyes. "I'm so sorry," she said. "I ate bread!"

I chuckled and told her to close her eyes again. My hands worked in tandem with an unseen helper. A sort of spiritual surgery transpired. I thought, *Something special is happening here.* My hands pulled energy knots, tossed invisible debris into my imagined flushing vortex on the floor. Energy pulsed, cleansed, and repaired.

After a few minutes, the intense energy dissipated. The strange coolness gave way to the natural heat of the day.

"Did you feel that?" I asked Joan.

She couldn't report anything special. Yes, she'd felt the energy and it had been relaxing, but nothing momentous.

There I stood amazed, and she was business as usual. She paid me and went on her way. Meanwhile, my ghost pain lasted a couple of hours. I shrugged my overheated self, *Well, that was really weird.*

As it turned out, weird, but wonderful.

The next evening I received an email from her. "Oh my gosh, I have been eating at a buffet--beef, shrimp, noodles, cake, donuts!"

Over the next weeks, Joan went on an eating frenzy, all the forbidden foods of the past fifteen years. "I may even try my old nemesis--ice cream!"

I advised her that would be a mistake. Asian people are often genetically lactose intolerant. I doubted the healing session included a complete altering of her DNA.

Later she concurred, "You were right about the ice cream."

Still, her ability to eat a much wider variety of foods brought her great joy and excitement.

Past Life Connection

Needless to say, we were both amazed by her healing. Feeling and seeing the angelic presence had been personally astounding, but then to hear about the results filled me with wonder, and still does.

For Joan, the healing was the beginning of a full life transformation on many levels. In many ways, her development had been arrested at age 23 when the condition struck. Her perennial college student look was an outward manifestation of her whole life.

At her next Reiki session we discussed if her situation could have some sort of past life connection. My personal illnesses chronicled in *Ever-Flowing Streams: Christ, Reiki, Reincarnation & Me* were ultimately resolved when the past life connection was revealed through Reiki treatments.

I was standing at her head as she lay on the table, discussing the possibilities. She said, "Can you see anything?"

I was about to say, *I don't do that sort of thing*, when a movie began to play in my mind. I saw a young Asian woman in a dark, dank prison cell. She was chained to the wall, starving to death. She had been a high born person of the nobility, but had been thrown into prison over political intrigue. She was cold, sick, angry, and dying.

I told Joan what I was seeing and it resonated with her. Possibly the woman had been 23 at the time. It's common for conditions connected with past lives to manifest at the age a person was when a critical event occurred.

In my case, I became ill with mononucleosis and the swelling neck glands associated with that disease at the age of nine. I continued to suffer swollen neck gland attacks for another forty years until Helen identified a child being sacrificed by a knife slice to the neck and a blow to the head in a Mayan lifetime. After my first session with Helen, I never experienced another attack. I needed healing in other areas, but that was a significant leap forward.

Joan, likewise, received a major boost during that angelic session that released her from "prison." At a followup session, I went through a whole visualization of healing that young girl. No longer a dirty, starving prisoner, she appeared clean and free. Lovely, dressed in a traditional Korean rich yellow brocade dress, she was smiling, fully restored, walking up a grassy knoll.

Joan's personal growth and transformation continues. We share a bond of friendship and wonder at this amazing thing called--energy healing.

Chapter Three ~ Attunements

July 10, 2011 ~ Supernal Friends Journal

Paula received an energy flow that seemed like a golden, heavy liquid. She walked over to Sue and me and "poured" it into our hands. We each felt a sensation of tingly heat and an increase of energy. Paula sat down and told us three entities were continuing to give us energy infusions.

The above journal entry was just one instance of a spontaneous attunement received during one of our living room Supernal Sessions. What exactly are "attunements?" Simply put, attunements are adjustments to a person's subtle energy field by a spiritual force. In the Bible, the disciples receive the Baptism of the Holy Spirit while hiding from the Roman authorities in an upper room after Christ's crucifixion and ascension. In Acts, the Holy Spirit comes in like a rush of wind and something like a flame is seen hovering above the heads of the men and women in the room. They are overcome with joy and accused of being drunk early in the morning. They speak new languages and rush out to begin their life-calling ministries, despite certain danger and possible death. That was one major attunement, or anointing, as it might be termed in Christian vernacular.

My first encounter with the word "attunement" was through the introduction of Reiki. Each level of Reiki involves receiving a different attunement. The origin of modern Reiki is traced to a Japanese man born in the middle of the 1800,'s--Mikao Usui. Legend has it that he was versed in both Christian and Buddhist traditions. Whatever his background, it is clear he had a heart for healing. At a certain point in his life, he reached a spiritual crisis and embarked on a three week retreat of meditation, fasting, and prayer on Mt. Koriyama in Japan. Diane Stein describes the first Reiki attunement in her landmark book, *Essential Reiki*:

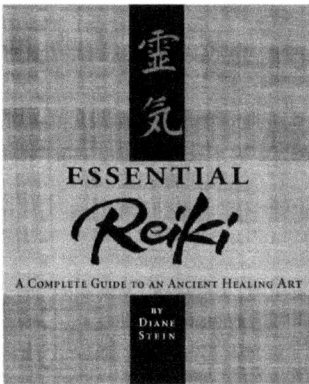

On the final morning of his quest, in the darkest hour before the dawn, Usui saw a projectile of light coming toward him. His first response was to run from it, but then he thought again. He decided to accept what was coming and the answer to his meditation, even if it resulted in his death. The light struck his third eye and he lost consciousness for a time. Then he saw "millions and millions of rainbow bubbles" and finally the Reiki symbols as if on a screen. As he saw each of the symbols, he was given information about each of them to activate healing energy. It was the first Reiki attunement, the psychic rediscovery of an ancient method.

Attunements are key to moving up the Reiki ladder. There are three basic levels in Reiki and moving from one to another is achieved by having a Reiki Master administer an attunement on the Reiki student. (Fortunately, students don't have to wait for a spontaneous bolt of spiritual lightning.) There are many teachers instructing students in the ways of Reiki, but at the end of day, receiving an attunement with the accompanying symbol is what it's all about.

Again quoting from Diane Stein in *Essential Reiki*:

The attunement process may be the most profoundly sacred thing on Earth today...The attunement turns on the light in a darkened house, reconnecting capabilities once universal but now mostly lost. The attunements heal our broken DNA, reconnecting us to the "Light" of the information that has been lost to Earth's people.

Supposedly once you receive an attunement, it can never be taken back. Your energy field forever holds that symbol and frequency in the aura. I have no idea how many attunements I have received over my lifetime. My first such experience came in 1983 in my bedroom in Oklahoma, when I received what Christians identify as the Baptism of the Holy Spirit.

Alone in my room, after months of prayer and spiritual seeking, I had a very real encounter with the Living Christ. The incredible feeling of agape love was a mountain top experience for me. I was forever changed. The catch phrase back then was "Born Again," taken from Jesus' discourse on spirituality in the Book of John and made popular by the spiritual memoir of Charles Colson. Jesus said one must be born in spirit to enter the kingdom of heaven. Was he talking about what happens after we die? Or, was he revealing a spiritual growing process in the midst of our earthly journey?

Over the past ten years, spontaneous attunements have become common place for the Supernal Friends. I think of each event as receiving another note on my energetic piano. There are 88 keys on a piano, each one has a unique pitch. Every attunement represents a unique frequency, like filling in the notes of a chord. Sometimes as I am working with a client on the Reiki table, it feels like I am switching frequencies. It's as if I have been turned into a healing instrument and transmit various frequencies as needed. This is all very intuitive and I certainly couldn't teach a course on "switching frequencies," but that's what it feels like. Some people believe that a Reiki session is always an attuning process; adjusting the energy levels of the client.

"Attunement" is such an appropriate word, because spirit is tuning us as surely as a piano tuner adjusts the strings on a piano to exactly the right pitch.

April 28, 2013--*Supernal Friends Journal*

I felt impressed to open my house this Sunday morning for a "Spiritual Salon." Paula knew she had to come to give everyone a special attunement. (Five women attended)...Before the meditation time began, Paula asked all of us if we were willing to accept the attunement. Everyone said yes. She laid down on the couch. We all quietly went into meditation on our own...After around 20 minutes, Paula sat up, eyes closed. She marched from person to person and gave us each an attunement. Her hands rested on our heads and then she traced some very specific symbols on our palms. Her thumb pushed firmly on pressure points under each finger. She brought our palms together to complete the attunement.

The frequency felt very "loving." The attunement seemed to go straight into my heart chakra. My head felt very light and open...As I sat on the couch, my arms moved very slowly on their own, following some sort of pattern. I was aware of being in the living room, but also could see cliffs in my mind's eye, like the hills around Sedona. It felt like being two places at once. Sue was the first to rouse out of the meditation. I had a very difficult time opening my eyes and getting back to the present reality. After giving the attunements, Paula laid back down on the couch, having moved around the entire room with her eyes closed. She was the last to come back to the group. As often happens, she thought she had fallen asleep and had no memory of giving us the attunements at that time. She later confirmed it was a high 'love' frequency."

We went to lunch and all were extremely tired later in the day.

Attunements appear to be the process of raising our frequencies so we can better communicate with spirit and exhibit psychic gifts. Paula always had flashes of keen intuition, instructive dreams, and a heart for healing. But, it was only after receiving Reiki attunements and other healing modality frequencies that her talents turned into skills. Her ability to send distance healing and hone in on physical and emotional issues of people miles away is a result of study, practice, and attunements.

The Reconnection

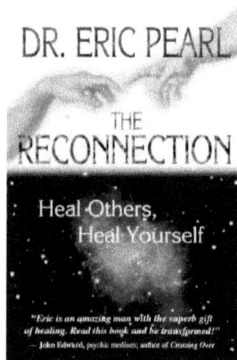

DR. ERIC PEARL

THE
RECONNECTION

Heal Others,
Heal Yourself

"Eric is an amazing man with the superb gift of healing. Read this book and be transformed!"
— John Edward, psychic medium; author of Crossing Over

In 2006, Sue, Paula, and I attended a lecture by Dr. Eric Pearl, known for his healing method called *The Reconnection.* As Dr. Pearl spoke, one of his assistants quietly walked around the room giving each of us the Reconnection Attunement. On the surface, she didn't appear to be doing very much. We each held our hands in front of us, palms touching. She held her hands over ours for a few seconds and then moved on.

I didn't feel any differently at the time, no lightning bolts, no heavenly winds blowing through my hair. However, when I went to bed that night, my body was very jerky. Most people have been awakened by a sudden movement of legs as they are drifting to sleep. It's a common reaction to the change in brainwaves as we move into the sleep mode.

My post-Reconnection attunement energy jolts were different. For one thing, I was not all that close to sleep. As I relaxed, energy in my abdomen seemed to shoot out in short bursts. For the first few days, it was rather alarming, all this jerking as I was trying to settle down to sleep. That was the disconcerting side effect of the attunement, which fortunately dissipated as my body adjusted to the new frequency.

The more encouraging and exciting result was an increase in my healing sensitivity. At the time, I was working daily as the caregiver of a stroke victim named Jean. I ran Reiki energy almost daily to help Jean with pain control. After the Reconnection attunement, my hands became instruments of much finer sensitivity. Yes, they still got warm, as most healers' hands do, but they also zeroed in on where her body was not functioning well. My palms now "buzz" over "hot spots."

Dr. Pearl teaches about the strands of energy in the auric field. These tangled strands became very real to me. In my mind's eye they appeared like knots of energy needing to be untangled, much like a rat's nest of electrical yarn. My therapy technique changed as I pulled and untwisted the invisible strands. There was a clear demarcation before and after the Reconnection Attunement with my healing abilities. The energy jolting still happens occasionally when I am sending long distance energy and those sessions often have very tangible results.

The Most Memorable Attunement

Sue once asked to me, "Do you know what I think has been the most amazing Supernal experience?"

I threw out a couple of guesses. "The time Edgar Cayce showed up in your living room?"

She shook her head. "That one's close."

I guessed again. "The soldier ghost at the Santa Fe Cemetery that Paula sent to heaven?"

"Nope," she said. "The time our hands glittered."

I have to agree that was pretty darned amazing.

November 11, 2011--We gathered in my living room, per usual. The meditation seemed intense from the beginning. Paula slumped into unconsciousness almost immediately. Sue began hearing messages, some made sense, others seemed cryptic and puzzling. I felt the cool energy of my Blue Angel envelope me. My mind filled with many images. I even sensed a man sitting next to me, bald with a gentle, loving spirit. Paula later described the same person when she came back to our reality.

Forty-five minutes into all of this, Paula asked in an uncharacteristically commanding tone, "Are you ready? The divine of the highest order is ready to give you an opening. Will you accept it?"

Sue and I exchanged a shrug. In for a penny, in for a pound. "Yes," we said.

With her eyes closed, Paula motioned for me to cross over to her. I lifted my hands, palms up in front of her. Without opening her eyes, she unerringly held one hand and then the other over my palms and traced very distinct symbols across them. During the meditation, I had been seeing a larger version of the symbols in my mind's eye. They were made of spokes of silver light. She pressed my palms together. I returned to my seat. Sue then received the same attunement.

After we had both returned to our seats, Paula lifted a palm and seemingly sealed the energy with three distinct pushes of her flat hand towards both of us.

She then slumped down again and slowly came to full consciousness. Sue and I sat mute, watching her transform from some Heavenly Messenger to our familiar Paula.

Paula blinked in amazement. "My gosh, there is sparkling light coming from all of our hands. Can you see it?"

Sadly, I couldn't see anything out of the ordinary and neither could Sue. But, Paula was still functioning at a higher level and witnessed the shining light, the man next to me, my angel and assorted other visitors. (It was a full house that day.)

As we all shared our experiences of the previous hour, I went to the kitchen and prepared a light lunch. We gathered around my dining room table. The sun streamed into the room and beamed onto the table.

Sue glanced at her palm in the sunlight and did a double take. Her hand was glittering. Little golden flakes appeared to be embedded in her skin.

She showed us, "Look!"

"What's that?" I asked. "Did you spill glittery eye shadow on yourself?"

"No."

Then Paula and I looked at our palms. They were glittery also! We stared at our hands and watched the glitter effect seem to rise up from inside our bodies. Sue's glitter even traveled up her arms. The longer we gazed, the more we could see. It was simply amazing.

We're grateful we have each other to share these experiences. Otherwise we might seriously doubt our sanity. We know the outside world might indeed wonder about our mental health, but at least we'd be put into the funny farm together.

The glitter effect lasted for several days. How that attunement has affected us, I do not know. In September of 2013 Sue reported waking up one morning with the "glitter effect" across her forehead. I wonder what her sleeping self had been doing that evening?

As it turns out the "glitter effect" is not unique to the Supernal Friends. A "chance" conversation with some evangelical Christian friends brought up the "gold dust" phenomena seen in some charismatic churches across the world. Miraculous healings and gold dust appearing on people have been reported in Brazil and United States, even going so far as to manifest on floors and pews. One such experience is related in the article *Gold Dust From Heaven* at Christian-Faith.com.

The glitter effect is a beautiful manifestation of Spirit's light and love.

The Dolphin Attunement

May 2013--Sue called and said, "Um...I know this will sound strange."

"What else is new?" I replied.

"I've been told to come over to your house and give you an attunement."

"Okay. I'll finish vacuuming. Come on over."

Sue seemed slightly spooked by feeling guided to administer an attunement. She'd also felt compelled to search through her stone collection and lit upon one to use as conduit for the frequency. Interestingly, she chose a sparkly pyrite that glittered and reminded us of the time our hands had sparkled after our "glitter effect" attunement.

We went back to my Reiki Room and I laid down on the massage table. (It's nice to be the receiver of a treatment once in a while.) I closed my eyes and relaxed. Sue opened up her channels and moved around me, following intuitive instructions. I didn't pay much attention. One thing I do remember is her touching the top of my feet with the golden stone.

Soon, a vision began playing in my mind. *In water...ocean water...swimming...water sliding along my body...dolphins all around... I am a dolphin.* (Mind split, partly observing, partly experiencing.) *Core power in my dolphin body...twisting...turning....part of the pod. Dolphins all around...joined mentally. Little sense of individuality...part of the whole. Speed...waves...air...freedom...*

Wow, was that cool! I'm not sure what happened in that attunement, except it seemed like I really connected with dolphin energy. Water sluicing down my body was a new, joyful sensation, the strength and speed exhilarating. Losing my sense of individuality was also very different. Humans have strong egos. We are always separate from those around us. The dolphin "me" had little sense of separation from the others. We were of one mind. Fascinating.

Some people believe dolphins are more highly evolved spiritual creatures than humans. Their brain is large and they are clearly intelligent. They have a sonar language, play games, and have been known to rescue people and even dogs. Channeled messages through Lee Carroll by the entity known as Kryon credit dolphins and whales with holding Akashic records for the planet and working closely with the spirit of the earth called Gaia.

I've always had a great affinity for water, especially the ocean. Almost every picture I've ever purchased for decoration has had a water theme. I swim twelve months of the year. When vacations or family emergencies keep me away from a pool for very long, I feel deprived and stiff. Water feels like home.

Still, becoming a *dolphin* is a bit of stretch, even for metaphysical little old me. I've never displayed a dolphin fetish. *A Dolphin's Tale* is not my favorite movie. I haven't yearned to join Greenpeace and fight off Japanese fishermen to save the dolphins.

On the other hand, I do find myself praying for the oceans quite often, sending healing energy into the depths. The health of the planet depends upon the health of the sea. Maybe the dolphins are doing their best to heal the water also. I don't know.

As I write these words, the dolphin attunement is still a fairly recent development. We'll see if it has some connections down the road. My younger daughter arrived for a visit a couple of weeks after the attunement bearing gifts.

She said, "A guy made these shirts and gave them to me. I thought they looked like you."

She was right--one pink, one turquoise, one black--all with an artful rendition of a dolphin. I've been wearing them all summer.

After Effects of Attunements

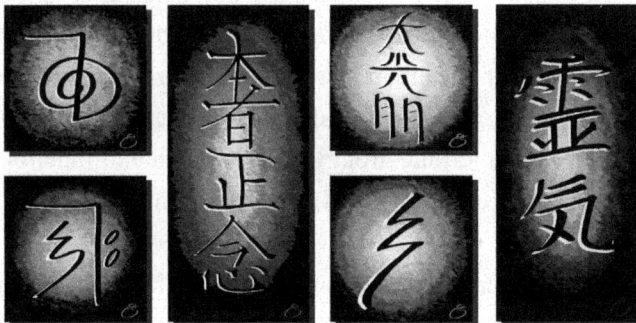

Are attunements something to fear? Years ago when I was contemplating taking my first Reiki class, a conservative Christian friend warned me, "Don't let them do any of those symbols over you."

He knew next to nothing about Reiki, but symbols have been associated with witchcraft, black magic, and sorcery. The bad guys. Of course, our world is rife with symbology. Every company designs a logo -- a symbol of their identity. Every currency in the world is stamped with symbols. Reiki symbols have Japanese roots, names, and healing attributes. The spontaneous attunements we've received have generally also come with symbols also. Their meanings have not been revealed to us. We have always been asked if we would receive the attunement and we've granted permission.

At this point, I never think twice about accepting an attunement from either Paula, Sue or Helen. Why? Because I am a much higher functioning person than I was before I ventured on this Reiki road. In some ways I barely recognize the person I am now compared to the person I was ten years ago.

My struggles were common:

• Depression ~ never knowing one day to the next if it would be a "good" day or a "bad" day. I was never "clinical," but sadness covered me like a blanket.

• Sleep Deprivation ~ Every insomniac knows the frustration of being exhausted and yet, wide awake. When everyone else in the house was enjoying sweet dreams, I roamed around the house in the middle of the night. I tried all the tricks--exercise, reading, music, pills, alcohol. Whiskey was my best late night friend. Shallow sleep left me groggy and barely able to function. I'd think back on a week and tick off the few nights I could call a "good night's sleep."

Ten years later, those issues have melted away. Attunements lifted me in increments. I no longer live at the frequencies of depression, insomnia, and alcohol dependency. I still enjoy a glass of wine, but whiskey and I have parted ways.

Benefits of Attunements

• Physical and emotion healing ~ Many conditions simply improve. I have an unproven theory that diseases have certain frequencies. Attunements will alter a person's vibrational frequency so that they no longer exist within the frequency of various disorders. That's my best guess regarding the mechanics of how attunements impact physical ailments.

• Enhanced psychic gifts ~ For myself the increased ability to help people heal came as a surprise. I honestly didn't realize that was happening until strangers made their way to me for Reiki treatments. I was very leery at first that I could do anyone any good. But, surprisingly, the energy flowed and the information and guidance came. I like working on strangers now, because I have no preconceived ideas. They are a blank slate. The first treatments are often the most powerful, bringing insights and healings that, frankly, surprise me and the client.

Sue and Paula have also experienced the development of their gifts. Sue is increasingly clairaudient. She hears messages, music, and sometimes complete downloads of information. Paula sees and hears through the veil. She communicates with entities, spirits, and angels.

Healing is a process. I didn't have one certain attunement and never suffered from depression again. It was gradual and almost a side effect of the attunements. This is pure speculation, but seems as if Spirit (God, Jesus, Source, Divinity...) is training us and patiently attempting to raise our physical frequencies to engender better communication with the Divine. Attunements equip us for the spiritual business that is our true life's work.

Where Can You Get Attunements?

There are many teachers and healers working in a myriad of modalities. Many of them include performing attunements. Other names for attunements are "openings" and "initiations." Before embracing any of them, I would suggest prayer, meditation, and investigation. Reiki Masters are now in every state and many countries. Reiki treatments are given in hospitals, colleges, alternative health clinics, and spiritual centers. Let Spirit be your guide. If you feel more comfortable in Christian circles, charismatic congregations have healing services that can lead to anointings and being baptized in the Holy Spirit.

If you follow other traditions, you'll find the paths to Source if you really want to get there. My Buddhist friend feels spiritually awakened through chanting. The most important thing you need is a willing heart. The Creator will answer the invitation. *Knock and the door will be opened.* If you set your intention to grow closer to Spirit, guidance will appear. Attunements improve communication between humans and the Divine.

Chapter Four ~ Past Lives

Supernal Journals--September 17, 2008

I am given a session with a psychic healer in St. Louis by my daughter, Sara. The healer's name is Julie. She has me lie down on her therapy table. The walls of the room are draped with Eastern cloths. She places crystals on my chakras to balance them. She dings little chimes, then sits and writes what she "gets." I rest with my eyes closed and float into a gentle dreamlike state. Soon I see a dog's face--a wolf or a husky. Then I see "myself" as a Mongol male dressed in fur and mukluks standing with the dog on an icy mountain looking across a range of snow covered peaks, perhaps the Himalayas. I have a short, stocky, strong body. I look down and see my feet and fur-covered hands trudging through the snow. I have a sense the dog and I are going to a temple, high above some stone steps. I feel the crunch of the snow ratchet up my legs. It is a long, arduous trip. We are on a mission.

Do you believe?

People raised in a Judeo-Christian Western culture sometimes ask, "Do you believe in reincarnation?" as if it is a matter of faith, like "Do you believe in Christ or Mohammed, or Buddha?"

For me, that question is like asking, "Do you believe in gravity?" "Do you believe the earth is round?" At this point, reincarnation is simply the way the world works. My world, anyway.

Until 2005, reincarnation was simply a theoretical concept to me, an Eastern philosophy. My spiritual journey and healing from a lifelong affliction involved an understanding of past life influences in our present reality. The thread of that discovery weaves through *Ever-Flowing Streams: Christ, Reiki, Reincarnation & Me*. Since I have already written there about the history of belief in reincarnation in the West, I won't reiterate it here. Except to say there was a concerted political decision in the Catholic Church by the fifth century to obliterate the belief in reincarnation throughout Christendom. Until that time, there had been room for discourse. The Fifth Ecumenical Council of 553 A.D. condemned believers in past lives to destruction. An entire sect of half a million believers in France, the Cathers, were wiped out in the 1200s. Believing in reincarnation became a good reason to be burned at the stake to "purify" the soul.

Little wonder today that a residue of fear remains for anyone to proclaim an open mind to the reincarnation viewpoint within the confines of a Christian community. An excellent source of historical information about the relationship between the Christian church and reincarnation can be found at Carol Hubbard's website, *Reincarnation Truth*.

Certainly, the knowledge of reincarnation does not guarantee a civil society. Indeed, just as Christianity has been adulterated and twisted to rationalize racism, the Holocaust, and the Inquisition, so has reincarnation been a foundation for the caste system and other ways to keep people down. The Eastern interpretations of reincarnation and how they have shaped that world leave a lot to be desired, in my opinion.

I find no conflict between seeing the broader context of the human experience relative to past lives and my personal faith as a follower of Christ. I am grateful that I've lived in a culture in Southern California in the 21st century where I could explore ideas and not be burned at the stake. Certainly that is not the case across the globe. Where and when I was born was no accident.

Over the past thirty years, the idea of past lives having an impact on present lives has become a growing field of study largely due to the work and popular books of Dr. Brian Weiss (*Many Lives, Many Masters*) and Dr. Michael Newton (*Destiny of Souls* and *Journey of Souls*). Past life regression therapy is gaining respect in mental health circles. Some surprisingly dull books on a fascinating subject have popped up written by academic therapists.

After I came to peace with the entity that had seemingly dominated me through a past life connection, as related in *Ever-Flowing Streams*, my curiosity about past lives grew. Also, I had a couple of spontaneous past life memories. I believe they were part of my spiritual education.

You might think of them as dreams or visions, but they feel like memories. Memories are different from dreams. They have substance and point of view. Recall a moment from your childhood. Go back to a school yard incident. You remember it from the vantage of a younger you, with a child's mentality and physical size. As you do this from an adult's mind, you can conjure it up. The childlike feelings are layered with the awareness that time and maturity have given you. A past life memory feels very similar.

On a Distant Plain

I am a young Native American male from long ago. I am on a ridge looking over a vast plain of prairie land. Yellow stalks undulate to

the horizon. I look down at my hands and legs. They are wiry and very different from what I am currently accustomed to seeing. A short distance from me stands a pale horse. I love this creature and think of him as a friend and companion. My best friend. There isn't the sort of separation in my mind between man and beast that we have developed throughout the centuries. I don't have a complicated language or logical thinking. I don't consider the past or future much. Life flows. I am part of the surroundings. Nature is not something I visit. It is the essence of my existence. The earth begins to tremble and then shake. Clouds of dust herald thousands of buffalo stampeding across the plain. I stand with my friend, the horse, and watch.

In the next memory I am the same man, only now very old, thin, and weak sitting on a similar hill. My energy is sinking, as I drift towards death. A natural finish to that cycle of life.

As I've pondered that memory, I think I was shown where my love for nature began and my ability to live in the moment. My connection to the earth, my love of gardening and animals, all resonate to that memory. Being inside a house too long is depressing. Open air is revitalizing. I can savor the moments of life without worrying about the future or dwelling on the past.

It's fascinating to be inside the mind of a person who feels so essentially different from the person I am today. That young man seemed more animal than human. He reacted with primal instinct and experienced the world without the mind-chatter of a left-brained modern woman. And yet, that was also--me. A part of the whole....of me.

The Minister

I am walking along a country road in rural America, probably the Midwest, perhaps around 1800. I am an itinerant preacher and am returning home after making the long rounds to the towns in my assigned area. It is warm and dusty. The fields around me have tall grass and wild flowers. Off in the distance I see the familiar barn and I am so grateful to almost be home.

I am very tall. My arms are long and my feet fill dark, heavy shoes. The cloth of my man's suit is scratchy, but I am accustomed to it. A woman appears on the hill wearing a long dress of the period. She sees me and begins to run toward me, calling out. Four children of various sizes come over the rise of the hill, where our home must be. They trot toward me, happy and excited.

I am overcome with the joy of my family. My wife has dark hair and ivory skin. She is beautiful and kind. I am in awe that she could care for an unattractive, gangly man such as myself. The smallest of the children jump on me and I raise one to sit on my shoulders. The wonder of having this happy family seems like a never-ending miracle for which I am very grateful. I gaze at my wife and feel incredibly honored that she is mine.

The emotion this memory brings forth in me, as I write, stirs me as deeply as thoughts of my present-day family. The feeling of being a tall, gangly man is such a contrast from the short woman I experience today. Once again, looking at hands and feet from inside the individual was startling. It was me and yet it wasn't me. The overriding feeling from that lifetime glimpse was gratitude for the blessing of family. I suppose I carry that with me today. The woman's face was clear in my mind; the children lesser so, although they all seemed to be fair with red hair. I thought myself unworthy to have such a lovely wife and happy children. They seemed like a blessing beyond measure from God.

Today, I relish being with my family. My daughters and grandchildren feel like a blessing beyond measure. Indeed, the physical bodies of the minister and me were very different, but we are linked at the soul.

Children with Long Memories

As we head into a new cosmic age, children are being born onto the earth plane with unprecedented mental abilities. They have been dubbed Indigo Children, Star Children, and Crystal Children. Some of these newcomers appear to remember a past life. This phenomenon is well documented in the East, where reincarnation is the accepted philosophy. Canadian-born Professor Ian Stevenson developed groundbreaking research by traveling across the globe to investigate reported instances of children remembering past lives. Roy Stemman chronicles fascinating examples of these children in *One Soul, Many Lives* and *The Big Book of Reincarnation.*

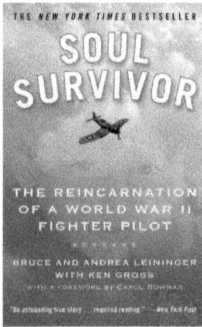

Now, the West appears to be seeing more children relating past lives, much to the amazement and concern of their parents. The Leininger family of Lafayette, Louisiana have written their story in the riveting tale, *Soul Survivor*. At the age of two, James Leininger began having nightmares of an airplane battle. He screamed "Airplane crash! Plane on fire! Little man can't get out!" As little James grew, his recounting of a life as James M. Huston, Jr., a World War II pilot was vivid with detail.

Texas born Bruce Leininger, James' father, was not raised in a culture that accepted a reincarnationist world-view and set out to find another explanation for his son's information. He embarked on a journey that ultimately led to the U.S. Navy carrier *Natoma* that confirmed the family and friends of the pilot who died a half-century earlier. While Bruce was dealing with the remembered details, his wife,

Andrea, was more concerned with helping her young son come to terms with a traumatic past life and move on to a happy present life.

More cases of apparent past-life connections are featured on a documentary series called, *The Ghost in My Child*. Besides featuring James Leininger, one episode found a girl who remembers being killed in the Oklahoma City bombing and a boy who recalls the plane hitting the World Trade Center and his death, falling to the pavement and then being covered with the building debris.

These children all remember violent deaths. This is often the case with these spontaneous recollections. It's as if the people felt they had much unfinished business and were totally surprised by their deaths. They often want to go home to their former families.

In *Soul Survivor*, Andrea Leininger sets an excellent example of realizing the need for closure for her child. Once she gets all the facts of where her son "died," the family takes a trip to the place in Japan where the air battle occurred. Flowers are strewn into the sea and the pilot is given a proper memorial and goodbye. James Leininger lets go of the past to live the new life before him.

Helping Children Dealing with Past Life Recall

Parents confronted with a child speaking of other times and places can be confused and dismayed. Having a toddler screaming in the night from horrific dreams is heartbreaking. Handling a child unusually precocious who doesn't fit in with classmates is challenging.

Fortunately, sources are emerging to provide guidance and therapy for struggling families.

Carol Bowman

One pioneer in the West helping people deal with children who remember past lives is Carol Bowman. After her children both recalled violent deaths, she came to realize that parents need help nurturing these unique children. Her book and website *Children's Past Lives* is a good resource for people struggling with the shadows of the past.

Jim B. Tucker, MD

Dr. Jim B. Tucker worked as the assistant to Dr. Ian Stevenson studying past lives through the Division of Perceptual Studies at the University of Virginia. After Dr. Stevenson retired in 2002, Dr. Tucker continued the research. As a family and child clinical psychologist, he works with families dealing with the stress of past life recall. His books, *Life Before Life* and *Return to Life,* chronicle case studies and his scientific investigations of this emerging phenomena.

Personal Mysteries

Most of us aren't dealing with children and past life nightmares, but many of us do have personal mysteries that cause pain, confusion, and stymie our growth. Why do we have unexplained fears? Chronic illness? Recurring bad relationships? Obsessions? Or on a more positive note, where did our talents come from? Why do we have certain affinities and tastes? Why are children from the same parents so vastly different?

Can reincarnation answer these questions? Is it necessary to delve into past lives? For most people, past lives are at best simply an interesting conjecture. Childhood memories and history of this life experience are enough to deal with.

However, for some people, taking a deeper look may be the key for living a happier, freer life. I lived over 50 years with anxiety and unexplained physical problems that went away over the course of time once the past-life connection was revealed. If I had been raised in a culture that considered past-life as the bigger picture, I might have discovered the connection much earlier. I'm grateful I finally connected the dots and worked my way to emotional and physical freedom.

Times are quickly changing. People struggling with persistent problems, patterns, and phobias can now find professional help and see into the depths of their souls.

Past Life Regressionists

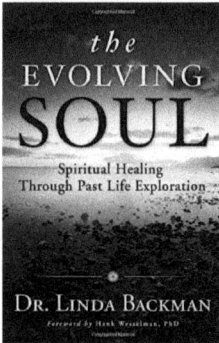

A growing field of therapy is past life regression hypnotherapy. I've sat through lectures of two leaders in the field, Dr. Linda Backman and Mira Kelley. Dr. Backman studied with Michael Newton and is the author of the book, *Bringing Your Soul to Light*. Her very professional demeanor makes you feel like The Doctor is Definitely In. She explains soul regression hypnotherapy at her website:

Soul Regression hypnotherapy is a mechanism or tool that allows an individual to access the memory of past lives and of the period when we are pure soul between lives. It is an experience of stepping back and forth, rather like a see-saw, from a place in current time where there is a past and a future into a timeless space where we are, and always will be, pure soul energy.

During soul regression hypnotherapy, we function simultaneously both in body and in the spiritual realm, experiencing our Higher Self, that holographic counterpart of our deepest essence that resides permanently in Spirit. During this encounter, we are gifted with the ageless and eternal knowledge of who we truly are ... pure soul.

Regression hypnotherapy is thus a powerful tool. In simple terms, it refers to the use by a trained practitioner of specific breathing techniques, guided imagery and other non-invasive means to guide the client into a natural state of relaxation or trance hypnosis that is conducive to accessing other than current life data.

Mira Kelley

Former lawyer, turned past life therapist and Hay House author, Mira Kelley, is leading workshops across the globe helping people connect to their past lives and the patterns, phobias, and challenges that may be connected to the present. Sometimes a personal mystery can only be resolved by seeking baggage we carried into the present existence from past life experience and figuring out how to unload it.

I drove to Santa Monica to get the Mira Kelley experience in person. The five hour workshop took place in a yoga studio with a very hard wooden floor. We brought our own yoga mats, which we sat upon, did I mention, for FIVE hours. On a hardwood floor.

Anyway, Mira Kelley was born in Eastern Europe and has a melodious, slightly accented voice. She was born to hypnotize. Her voice floats around the room, creating its own soothing energy. She spoke of her personal encounters with past life memories and how they affected her current life. Much of her talk is also related in an article on the Hay House website:

I regressed myself and I had a very dramatic experience. I saw myself as a Soviet spy during World War II. Working as a doctor was my cover. One of my patients was a very important Nazi general. I received orders to eliminate him. I felt that killing a man was not the right thing to do, yet it was of great importance for my country and for stopping an evil machine. I felt trapped and not seeing another option, I poisoned the general. I was quickly caught by the Nazis and was executed by an electric chair. I did not experience any pain or discomfort. I simply observed from above how at the moment of death, my spirit, which looked like white energy, lifted from the body. As my spirit was floating up, there was a great sense of serenity. In the black void a path of light appeared. There was a being of white light that awaited to greet my spirit. In that moment I knew that I would never be afraid of dying.

A question came from the recording I have made for myself, "What lessons did you have to learn?" Tears began rolling down my face as I felt the simplicity and the profound truth of the lesson: Be good; be loving. My first regression had a tremendous impact on my life. The need to be good and loving became of paramount importance to me. It even made me realize how appropriately my parents have named me. My full first name is Dobromira. It is a Slavic name composed of two words. "Dobro" means "good" and "mir" means "peace, world." Following my regression, I chose to be someone who brings good to the world.

In my late 20s, regression powerfully influenced my life again. As a result of some dental work, I developed TMJ in my jaw. Following a year of pain, during which I made every imaginable effort to heal it, my dentist suggested that I either have an operation or learn to live with it. Neither option seemed appealing. I was desperate for a solution. That is when I remembered the regression I did as a girl. I quickly found a practitioner.

During my regression, I saw myself as a slave. There was a metal collar around my neck. It was very thick and heavy. I had four manacles that were placed around my wrists and my ankles. A chain was attached to the collar around my neck and continued down to the manacles. The metal collar was always there and was very uncomfortable. It rubbed my jaw and I had a permanent wound right where the main pain spot on the left side of my face was.

This vision had a powerful correlation to where I was in my life at that time. It allowed me to process the issues I was facing and to see new possibilities on how to deal with the challenges. The experience was very cathartic for me. The following day, I woke up without pain in my jaw. My dentist called my healing a miracle.

These are two examples of the powerful emotional transformation and physical healing that people experience during regression. It also allows them to communicate with their Higher Self, spirit guides and angels, and receive guidance when making important decisions or receive answers to life-long questions. It assists them in obtaining clarity on their life's purpose. My clients are able to learn about their relationships with family members and close friends and what roles those people have played in other lifetimes they have shared with them. Gaining this understanding allows them to approach the relationships in present day with compassion, forgiveness and love.

Read more about Mira Kelley at her website and check out her book, *Beyond Past Lives.*

Quantum Healing Hypnosis Technique (QHHT)

Past life regression hypnosis was pioneered by therapist Delores Cannon in the 1970's. Cannon began as a trained hypnotherapist helping people break addictions to smoking and overeating. A spontaneous regression by a client to a 1920's flapper lifetime sparked an interest of investigation in Dolores. Married to a career US Navy man, she raised four children and traveled the world, until a serious auto accident confined her husband to a wheelchair for the rest of his life.

After they moved to Arkansas to lead a quiet life, Dolores was able to study the past life phenomena in depth. Over the course of time, she worked with thousands of clients and developed a system called Quantum Healing Hypnosis Technique (QHHT) that now has thousands of practitioners around the world. Cannon wrote and published many books detailing the past lives revealed by clients.

From delorescannon.com:

The first book was "A Soul Remembers Hiroshima" (1993), which reports the life of a man who describes his experiences as a Japanese man in Hiroshima in 1945 when the atomic bomb was dropped on the city in World War II. This shocking account of the dropping of an atomic bomb from the perspective of a person who was there provides a chilling lesson into the horrific effects of war and nuclear weapons. The second book was "Jesus and the Essenes"(1992), which describe the life of a young man who was an Essene teacher of Jesus. Many truths about Jesus himself, his personality, his background, his life and the times he lives in are revealed in this fascinating account of a teacher who describes her personal relationship with Jesus in loving detail.

Besides writing many more books as information developed, she established a company, Ozark Mountain Publishing, that features over fifty authors opening the boundaries of conventional thinking.

QHHT practitioners are working with people worldwide to reveal their personal mysteries and work toward mental, emotional, and physical healing. For more information visit: DoloresCannon.com

The Takeaway

Recalling past lives isn't necessary to live a full, satisfying present life. Dipping in the River of Forgetfulness before birth is a blessing, giving every baby a chance to explore life from a fresh perspective. Everything is new. Life is full of possibilities.

Yet, beneath the surface of consciousness, past life memories, tendencies, and imprints bubble up. Sometimes they present as an amazing talent, no explanation necessary. Other times they disrupt life, bring pain, or mystery. That's when delving into soul memory can be a healing tool towards a happier, healthier existence.

It's great to live in an age when we have the freedom to explore such possibilities.

Where are the Memories?

Our brains store our memories from this life. But why can't we easily recall past lives? Because they are not in our brains. They reside in our Akasha Field. That brings up the tantalizing subject of the Akashic Records.

Chapter Five ~ The Akashic Records

Supernal Journals ~ February 13, 2015 In meditation today I saw that humans come together as a blend of DNA not only of the mother and father, but there is a third component, a spiritual strand from the soul entering the physical body. There is an etheric DNA that weaves into the cells of the developing fetus as surely as the genetic material from the physical plane. This is the Akasha. It carries the past lives, traits, talents, memories, skills, and personalities of the lives that came before. Spiritual literature often refers to a "silver cord" attached to the body and soul. When the person dies the cord is disconnected. Akashic information is carried in the cord--spiritual DNA. The memories are not linear; they are not stored in the brain, but in the Akashic auric field. It's all somehow connected to a general Akashic field curated by the Guardians of the Records. I was given a vision of three twisting strands of DNA--one brightly shining of light energy--that go into forming a new human life.

Akasha is a Sanskrit word meaning sky, space, or aether. The Akashic Records are known as the Records of All Things. My understanding of the Akashic Records is constantly evolving. At first I pictured a beautiful, marble Library in the Sky that held a book about every soul ever born. A host of shining-robed Guardian Librarians roamed the gilded halls, being assigned to take care of certain areas and the souls represented. *Records on Dana Taylor? Third floor, row B.* That was my human mind coming up with a working metaphor.

Reading, learning, and connecting to the Akashic field has thrown that simplistic image out, yet I haven't really replaced it with a new one. The Akasha isn't a place "out there," it is a field of information that unites dimensions of reality. It is singular and yet universal. Much like individual people, who are all part of the human race, similar in countless ways, yet each is unique. No two humans are identical, not even twins. Akashic information plays a major part in creating that individuality. It is partly innate Akashic information that makes you uniquely you, along with the genetic material inherited from your biological parents.

Kryon Speaks

The most detailed information of the Akashic Field I've encountered comes from the channeled material from the entity Kryon through Lee Carroll. Carroll has been channeling Kryon for nearly thirty years. They are "partners." Through the years Carroll has compiled thirteen books from the material, linking session subjects together in a cohesive manner.

Lee Carroll

Information from sessions focused on the Akash, as Kryon likes to call it, has been gathered by Australian author Monika Muranyi in *The Human Akash: A discovery of the blueprint within.* Kryon offers a different metaphor for human understanding of the Akashic Field. Rather than a library, think of a huge cavern. Kryon calls it the Cave of Creation. Within that cave are countless crystals. Each soul is tied to a crystal of information--their personal Akashic Record. Beyond the Cave of Creation, there is something he calls the Crystalline Grid that covers the surface of the earth. It is all a part of the Akash--the Record of All Things. The Crystalline Grid holds the information of human events that take place on the land. For instance, empaths often pick up terrifying emotions on a battle field because they were imprinted on the Crystalline Grid. Haunted houses and places with "bad vibes" are all shimmering frequencies from the Crystalline Grid. Conversely, "sacred ground" throbs with high frequencies embedded in the Crystalline Grid from spiritual human activity. Every action and emotion is recorded in the quantum layers of the Akashic Fields--collectively upon the Crystalline Grid and individually in the personal crystal Akashic Record of every soul.

The previous paragraph boils down copious information into a few sentences. If you find the Akash intriguing, read the *The Human Akash.* Go to Kryon.com and listen to free podcasts of channeled sessions. Many are also on YouTube with titles for each session. Prepare to have your world view altered.

Kryon says Akashic information is encoded in our DNA. It explains why sometimes individuals feel they don't belong with their family. For instance, there may be five children born into a Mexican family. Four of them love the carne asada, frijoles, and chilis. The fifth gets indigestion and gravitates toward vegetables and fish. While the rest of family have incarnated in South America many times, the fifth child has been an Asian more often. The Mexican experience is new and sometimes feels odd, even the food is strange. Though the human DNA is similar between children, the Akashic DNA is very different from the other siblings. Human inheritance plays only a partial role in our complete genetic makeup. Intriguing idea, isn't it?

The Akashic Reader

How does one access the Akashic information? Hypnotherapy and past life regression is one method. In that instance, the client is hypnotized and led to "see" influential past lives, while a therapist guides them through the process.

Another method is having an Akashic Records reading by someone trained and gifted in that area. Practitioners all have their own way of working, though many are schooled through the methods passed down by Ernesto Ortiz. His book, *The Akashic Records,* is a basic how-to for his technique.

Helen, whose website is *Ripples of Light,* has been my preferred Akashic Records reader. She opens the session with the prayer as presented in the Ortiz material. She is then able to receive information from the Guides of the Akashic Records. Who or what exactly these Guides are, is open to debate. At any rate, sessions begin by asking from a list of written questions prepared by the client. Helen's information seems to be a combination of Akashic information and mediumship.

Relatives or friends often pop in when they realize the line is open when Helen is doing a reading.

One Big Ball of Yarn

I once asked Helen if I had been a nun. "Yes," she said. "I see you in various forms of religious service. I see one life where you were in a dark monastery. You were treated harshly. They didn't understand the love of God at all. I see you scrubbing stone floors."

Figures. I am a cleaner. A scrubber. I definitely have a thing about floors.

Sitting in Catholic churches, drinking in the atmosphere, can feel quite sublime, though in this lifetime my church exposure has been of many Protestant flavors. My emotions toward the Catholic hierarchy are mixed. I attribute that to Akashic links in perhaps not-so-pleasant incarnations. *Inquisition, anyone?*

Of course I asked her about past lives with my husband. Helen said, "You were a nun and he was a priest. You couldn't really be together in that life the way you wanted to be, so you planned to be married in this one. I also see you as his student in another life. You were infatuated with him, but he didn't notice you in any special way."

I asked once about pre-life planning and if we determined our own course. Her metaphorical answer made me smile. "It's more like you are a string of yarn. When you come onto the earth you get wound into a large ball of yarn--all the strings of everyone else's lives combine. You are each separate and yet tied together."

Life is just one big ball of yarn!

A Movie in Her Mind

Lois J. Wetzel

Lois J. Wetzel, author of *Reincarnation: Past Lives and the Akashic Record* and *Akashic Records: Case Studies of Past Lives*, goes into a fully conscious trance state for her Akashic Records readings. She remembers what she sees for about a day, and then it fades like a dream. Her first reading was a spontaneous one which occurred a couple of years after she had a particularly profound dream in which the Archangel Gabriel gave her a copy of the Akashic Records. Her client asked if she could do past life readings and her first thought was that she could not. Yet she immediately realized that at some point the knowledge of how to do that had been downloaded to her. She happened to be standing at the head of the client when he asked about a past life. She believes that the link to the past lives is at the lower back occipital area of the brain. Somehow, she knew exactly what to do.

Lois receives a sort of psychic movie. She must keep narrating the story she sees or the action freezes. Her sessions are all recorded. If she is doing a long-distance reading, she will visualize the client lying on the table as she holds her hands behind his/her head.

Soon, she is linked to the most important past lives affecting current situations and patterns. These sessions require a tremendous amount of energy from Lois. She has to limit her sessions or suffer the consequences of exhaustion. Why does she do it? From *Reincarnation: Past Lives and the Akashic Record:*

I do these readings to heal the clients. Many times, there is injury or damage or "scar tissue," for want of a better term, affecting Souls as a result of occurrences in other lifetimes. When we are not in the body, the Soul does not experience the effects of this damage. It is only while we are incarnated in a body that the issues bother us, and to the best of my understanding, that is the only time we can heal them as well--when we are incarnated in a body.

Full readings generally include four to six lifetimes. She provides a detailed picture of surroundings, personalities, and events. At the end, the life lesson involved is revealed. For example, one incarnation recalled for a woman named Sandy took place in a beautiful society before our recorded history. Sandy's toddler son drowned in a shallow pool because Sandy was not paying adequate attention. The life lesson:

This event happened to teach her compassion, among other things. Sometimes children come in to live a short while to teach those around something. This kind of thing is agreed upon by everyone involved before incarnating. For Sandy, there is a recurring pattern in many of her lifetimes of either being a child who dies due to not being cared for properly, or being the parent who fails to supervise adequately. One of her lessons at a Soul level has been learning the importance of watching small children "like a hawk," as they say, and taking responsibility for their fragility when young....This Soul was learning compassion for people who make mistakes, and has now learned this on a Soul level.

Lois' popular books provide a wonderful glimpse of how past relationships and events influence emotions, phobias, talents, and passions of the present. The life lessons help clients get the bigger picture of their human experience. Clients can move beyond feeling victimized by betrayals, tragedies, disappointments and even illnesses. As the wise man said, *everything happens for a reason.*

Mining My Personal Akash

Look Within, as the saying goes. I consider myself a spiritual explorer rather than a gifted psychic. I have tendencies rather than obvious talents. I don't see dead people. I don't do psychic readings. Yet, I have experienced enough multidimensional phenomena to know there is much more around us than our five senses reveal. In fact, our senses are actually filters. If we could hear every sound wave or see every dust mote, we'd be in chaos. Our senses help us make "sense" of our existence. They create a limited reality to navigate our daily lives.

Meditation allows us to expand our perceptions and tap into more fields of information. After reading Ernesto Ortiz' book on the Akashic Records, I decided to give it shot. I'd see if I could peek into my personal history or connect with the wisdom of the Guardians. I would "mine my Akash," as Kryon puts it.

On Sunday mornings I devote extra time to mediation and prayer. I follow the protocol for opening the Akashic Records. A journal and pen are ready to write down impressions, visions, snippets of words. Some weeks I don't seem to get anywhere. Other times the spiritual adventures have been quietly exciting. Keeping the journal is essential because the information floats away like the remnants of a dream. On the other hand, some of the images still feel very real. Here are a few examples:

Supernal Journals-

August 5, 2013

Begin the morning doing Tai Chi. When I open the Akashic Records the intensity of the crown chakra opening is much greater. It is very difficult to open my eyes. It's like going into a tunnel. I speed past many people, objects, planes of time.

After a few minutes a sailing ship of the 1600's comes into focus. I am a teenage boy working onboard. Many images--the ship, the decks, the sea, winds blowing, rope everywhere. I feel the roughness of the rope, see it crossed and configured. The ship is big, overwhelming. Huge crates are fastened down by the rope. I see the upper deck with the steering wheel. Sometimes I sleep in a hammock dangling under the rafters below deck. I prefer sleeping on the open deck nestled in the curve of the hull toward the front of the ship. I feel the forward, undulating motion; hear the creaking of the ship, as if it is alive.

I admire the captain from afar. Try to keep a low profile, not be noticed. I climb the ropes. I may have broken my leg in that life.

We stop at an island. Beautiful tropical setting. I am in a row boat with others going to forage for supplies. I climb a coconut tree and cut green ones from high up with a heavy knife. I am skinny, quiet, and try to stay out of trouble.

I was shown this mainly as an exercise in developing my abilities to see past lives.

These trips to other "me's" fill me with wonder. In my current incarnation, I could no more climb a coconut tree than flap my arms and fly to the moon, yet there is a resonance of sensory memory--the rough ropes, the undulating ocean, chopping at the coconuts with all my strength. I feel an echo of all those moments. The boy is part of my Akash. I am he and he is me. But, he is not *all* of me.

Wisdom from Beyond

At other times, I have posed questions, rather than seeking glimpses of past lives. Opening the Akash includes connecting with higher intelligence. What is it? Higher Self, Angels, God, ET's? Some would say evil, but I've never sensed anything malevolent. In fact, my meditative states feel like encounters with Love Energy, ranging from a happy glow to blazing bliss.

The Ortiz book suggests asking a variety of insightful questions. So often we don't recognize our personal bugaboos. As Shakespeare said, *Know Thyself.* Sometimes it takes a little heavenly help.

Supernal Journals ~
September 15, 2013

What ancestral tie or what pattern has been established that needs to be cleared or changed?

Fear is a basic condition of humans that is a strong influence on all your reactions and plans. Fear-based theology, fear about health, wealth, war, invasion, personal safety, fear for children, fear of the future.

Come to recognize how much fear has influenced your life and see it as a bad habit to be broken. Break the ties and bondages of fear. Be liberated from all fear that has generally ruled humanity.

Seek the higher energies and allow them to dissolve the lower energies of fear. From that will come creativity, freedom, and joy. Higher entities will be attracted to you and aid you in your creative endeavors.

Messages from angels in the Bible often say, "Be not afraid. Fear not." These messages are not just for the past, but a permanent exultation to recognize fear as a crippling illusion. Shatter the illusion of fear and step into the light and love of the Christ.

I hadn't thought of myself as a particularly fearful person, though my daughters would beg to differ. Mothers are the nags of caution. *Don't go near the edge! Wash your hands to keep from getting germs! Don't talk to strangers! Wear sunscreen! Don't eat GMO's!* Keeping our children safe from lurking dangers is a mother's job. But perhaps we overdo it.

Reading that message made me realize how much fear is a habit. It limits our options, keeps us from taking chances. Closes us in a safe box of our own construction. I realized the wisdom of those words for my own life decisions. Now, when making life decisions, I consciously determine whether unreasonable fears are holding me back. I especially like the last line of the message--***Shatter the illusion of fear and step into the light and love of Christ.***

I may put that on a meme.

Standing on the Akashic Mountain

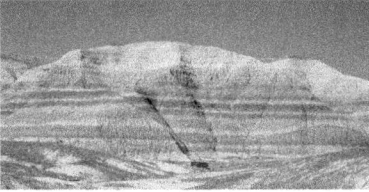

Perhaps the best metaphor for our personal Akasha Record isn't a library or a cave. Think instead of a cliff of sedimentary rock. As I've driven through the hills of Missouri, the roads wind between mountains cut for the highway. The exposed rock is composed of countless layers going back to millennia. Red, beige, brown, sparkling, or dull--each layer represents a geological era. Layer after layer compress to form a mighty mountain, covered with springs, grasses, trees, and flowers. Life scampers on the top, but each layer had its time in the sun.

We are all each our own little Akashic sedimentary hill, rising and growing with every life experience--the dark, the light, the sparkling, the dull. They are so tightly compressed we can barely tell where one layer begins and the other ends, but they all are part of us. Most of the time we are only playing on the top layer under the sun and the sky, but the firm foundation is below, ready to be explored.

Beyond that, our Akashic hill is just one part of the vast Akashic mountain range of humanity. We rise from Mother Earth, growing, ever changing, going on and on and on.

Embark on an archeological dig of your personal Akash. You may find buried treasure!

Chapter Six ~ Spirit Communication

Supernal Journals ~ September 26, 2010
Santa Fe, New Mexico--Supernal Friends vacation
Today we visited the Rosario Cemetery. Sue and I love exploring old cemeteries and reading the headstones. This one dates back to at least 1800. Paula opted to stay in the car. She doesn't like "walking on people's graves."

While Sue and I wandered around, Paula noticed a figure standing on the steps of the World War II Memorial. He was a soldier dressed in WWII battle clothing. At first she wondered if he might be part of a reenactment or publicity stunt. She watched him, fascinated.

Then she heard, telepathically, "Wow, you can see me."

She answered, telepathically, "Yes."

He replied, "Hey, could you help me out for minute?"

"Yes, I need for my friends to come back to the car."

She waited until we returned and asked us to give her a few moments because someone needed her help. She approached the steps of the memorial. The soldier appeared almost three dimensional to her.

He said, "People come here all the time, but nobody can see me. May I touch your hand?"

She lifted her hand and felt warmth. She said, "I know your name is James."

He nodded, "Yes, my name is James."

Paula looked at the rows of name plates glued to the marble base of the memorial. They represented the soldiers from Santa Fe lost during World War II. "What is your last name? There are a lot men named James here."

"James Moulton."

Paula followed the alphabet and touched the name of James Moulton. "Look, honey, here is your name. This is a memorial to you. You've passed."

She pointed out the statue. "This is a beautiful tribute to you and the other soldiers. What is the last thing you remember?"

"A huge, bright flash. I guess an explosion."

Paula said, "Why don't we have a prayer together?"

As she began to pray, power vibrated her whole body. Emotion swelled. She prayed that James be helped and guided home because he'd lost his way. He needed the Lord's loving guidance.

James looked up, "Wow, there's such a bright light coming from your prayer. Everything is getting really bright."

Paula couldn't perceive any difference in the light but asked him, "Where is it the brightest?"

He pointed.

She said, "That's where you need to go. That's where you belong."

James seemed unsure. "Can you hold my hand for a minute?"

"I will," Paula said. "They will be here to help you."

He picked up her hand as if to kiss it. He opened his arms and she stepped into a ghostly hug. Though she couldn't physically feel his body, she sensed his energy and his emotion. She wept softly, overcome with feelings of love, joy and sorrow.

Two souls touched.

She glimpsed him walk away and then disappear.

They're Not Dead, They're Nonphysical

Spirit communication took us by surprise. After Paula's "miraculous" healing of RSD in 2005, studying healing energy was our primary focus. As it turns out when you begin exploring multidimensional living, or *Supernal Living*, as I call it, you run into the entities that dwell there. Some of them are your relatives.

In fact, it appears that once people cross over, a bond remains with loved ones. Our soul family keeps in touch, coming in and out of our lives, as needed. At least that's how it appears, if personal experience is any indication.

After receiving Reiki attunements and other spontaneous attunements, both Sue and Paula made dramatic leaps in their ability to receive information, often uninvited.

Meddling Mothers

Sue's clairaudient gifts grew, despite her personal doubts. Twice my relatives intervened and wouldn't leave her alone until she took action. The first incident involved replacing the thirty-year old mattress I was sleeping on.

One day Sue called me. "You're going to think I'm nuts, but your mother has really been bugging me."

"Oh? What about?"

"She says you need a new mattress."

After my dad died in 2007, I moved into their bedroom and began sleeping on the mattress they'd purchased in the 1960's. Saggy, springs shot, it wasn't exactly sleeping on a cloud. Each morning I arose with lower back pain, bent over like an old woman. The stiffness took a couple hours to go away. Being a big cheapskate, I had no intention of buying a new one any time soon. Mattresses are expensive!

I related this to Sue. In her typical take-charge fashion, she declared, "We're going mattress shopping this weekend. I'll buy it. Your mother won't let it go."

"You're not buying me a mattress!"

The following weekend we went shopping. I purchased a wonderful mattress and paid it off over the course of a year. Money well spent.

In April of 2010, Sue received a strong impression that I was supposed to have a piano. This time it was my mother and Gramma Rose hounding her from beyond. She had a vision of me sitting at the computer. A big red X appeared across it, the message being I was spending too much time there.

They said I needed to bring music back into my life. A piano would provide beauty, joy, and peace. She saw me playing with ribbons of colored light coming out of the instrument.

Once again, I received a call. "Hey, it's me, Sue. Uh, your mom and grandmother are after me to get you a piano. Do you play the piano? I've never heard you play one."

I sighed. "Actually, I love playing the piano. I haven't had access to one for a long time, but as a kid I played all the old ballads of the 40's, 50's and 60's. I still have the sheet music. But, I can't afford a piano!"

Well, when your relatives from beyond are pulling the strings, miraculous things happen. I sold jewelry that had been stowed in a safety deposit box for decades. It paid for the piano and more. As events turned out in my life over the next couple of years, the piano provided escape and solace during some difficult times. Love my piano.

Medium Phobia

Talking to the dead is not favored in Christian circles. The Bible warns against it. A quick Google search to *BibleInfo.com* provides the many scriptures warning against mediums, spiritists, wizards, and sorcerers. Leviticus 19:31 NIV states *Do not turn to mediums or seek out spiritists, for you will be defiled by them.*

The sad tale of King Saul includes his desperate visit to the Witch of Endor, who supposedly conjures up the spirit of Samuel for guidance. King Saul meets his bloody end the next day.

New Testament references to mediums generally credit demonic possession as the source of the seer's extrasensory power, as in the story in Acts 16 when the Apostle Paul casts out an evil spirit from a slave girl being used as a fortune teller by her owners.

Raised with these warnings, I've steered clear of professional psychic mediums. Truthfully, many I've seen working fairs have turned me off. I once worked a Consciousness Expo. There were several psychics set up. By the end of the day, I thought of them as Dueling Psychics, each trying to out-psychic each other and grab clients at $50 a pop.

I had no desire to join the ranks of gullible people giving their hard earned cash to questionable psychic mediums. Worse than giving money was giving up personal power and putting faith in a fortune teller.

I believe that is the essence of the Biblical warnings.

Some of My Best Friends Are Mediums

Despite my religious upbringing, suddenly, my dearest, long time friends were communicating with nonphysical beings. This was new to them and me. One night on a trip to Colorado, Paula, Sue and I were sitting around a hotel room visiting. Paula had recently taken some advanced spiritual development classes and received what they called "openings," which raised her frequency.

She said, "Lately I've been seeing a sort of portal appear. The wall gets kind of wavy."

"What's there?"

She shrugged her shoulders. "I don't know." She looked across the room. "I'm seeing one now over there."

"Why don't you look through it?" I suggested.

Being in safe, supportive company gave her the courage to open the portal. That night was one of her first experiences of spirit communication. The recently departed aunt of a friend of mine appeared, offering him health warnings. He was experiencing heart issues.

After she went away, Paula said, "I'm hearing *My name is Ismael.*"

Sue and I sat up. I said, "That's my dad."

Paula frowned. "I thought his name was Dale."

A buddy in the Marine Corps decided my dad look like a *Dale*, and that became his name for the next sixty years. That night it became clear my dad was still taking an active role of helping me manage his household. He gave me permission to sell his 1967 Ford and cut down a favorite bush.

Sue joked, "Now that he's on the other side, he's taking the name that sounds more angelic--Michael, Raphael...Ismael."

As you can see, my personal encounters with my departed relatives have been about running day-to-day, mundane decisions of life. Yet, that is the stuff of life. It is comforting to think they are watching and helping.

She Sees Dead People

Paula's ability to see nonphysical beings with her eyes can be quite startling. Many mediums sense them in their mind's eye, but Paula can sometimes be confused by what appear to be 3-D individuals. She once thought she had hit someone with her car, until the person walked through her car and disappeared. On a cruise ship she saw a group of people dressed in period costumes and thought they were part of a show. She was about to point them out to her husband, but then they were gone. All of this has taken mental adjustments.

She has slowly developed a sense of mission in either helping people cross to the other side, or deliver messages to loved ones on this side.

In 2012, she and her husband took a cruise along the Mexican Rivera. Here is my entry:

Supernal Journals ~ September 2012

Paula and Wayne just returned from a cruise to Mexico. The trip was full of supernal surprises. It began with a room filled with negative energy. Paula got sick, had her back go out, and endured terrible nightmares. She finally realized it was a spiritual situation and called in the Christ spirit, her guides, and used essential oils to cleanse the space. After that, she felt much better.

Then on the decks, she began seeing the spirit of an old Mexican man. He only appeared when a rough-looking passenger, covered in tattoos, was in the area. The spirit nagged her to deliver a message to Mr. Tattoo. Paula was beyond hesitant. Shy by nature and intimidated by the size and scowl of the passenger, the absolute last thing she wanted to do was approach him with a dead person's message. Yet, the old man wouldn't leave her alone.

Finally, she saw Mr. Tattoo standing alone and gathered her courage. "I don't want to disturb you, but I have a message from E."

(Now, away from the moment, she can't recall the actual name, only that it began with an E.)

She continued, "If that name doesn't mean anything to you, I'll go away."

He stiffened and glared, but said, "What's the message?"

Taking a deep breath, she forged ahead, "He's saying you did the right thing. I see him holding a plug. He says you should stop feeling guilty. You are doing destructive things and you need to stop."

She also repeated some Spanish phrases, which she didn't understand. The imposing stranger looked visibly shaken. Tears welled in his eyes.

"Lady," he said, "I don't know who you are, but I've only cried twice in my life. Once when I had to shoot my dog and once when I had to give the order to pull the plug on my grandfather. Thank you."

Paula and the passenger parted company and never crossed paths again.

Paula is coming to terms with this multidimensional ability. Last year two men committed suicide in her circle of acquaintances. In both cases, they communicated with her after the events. She was given knowledge of missing objects and told where to find them. Rather than revealing where the information came from, she acted like she had a good hunch.

Spirit Communication is a talent that also requires discernment and discretion on the best way to handle the revelations received. Grief and loss are not a party games. Paula will incorporate her compassion, maturity, and generous nature as she continues to use her talents for the benefit of others.

Love Doesn't Die

My friend, Sylvia, is a professional, conservative business woman. Intuitive women run in her family. The occasional prophetic dream or premonition pops up now and then. Sylvia didn't devote any energy to studying psychic phenomena, being busy with her family, career, and community activities.

Then, she had a shocking, life changing experience. A close coworker, Maria, came into her office to discuss business. Sylvia noticed she looked tired and asked about her health.

Maria replied, "I've got a headache today."

She suddenly lost consciousness and fell from her chair onto the floor. Sylvia sat momentarily stunned as she witnessed Maria's spirit body, along with two little girls rise from the slumped body and ascend through the ceiling.

Sylvia yelled for help. Emergency medical help came quickly, but Maria had died instantly from a cerebral hemorrhage.

The event rocked Sylvia's world. She relived the moments seeing the strange images of the rising figures over and over. They looked something like old photographic negatives. What did it mean? What had transpired?

Sylvia began taking spiritual development classes. She attended lectures on everything from numerology, feng shui, spiritual art, energy healing, to spirit communication. She became one of my regular Reiki clients and sent me many referrals.

Once, when Paula, Sue, and I were giving her a Reiki treatment, Maria came through to Paula. She offered Sylvia a comforting message. Paula saw the image of a Christmas ornament. That turned out to be the last present Maria had given Sylvia.

Ultimately, Sylvia felt drawn to mediumship. Living in Southern California offered her the opportunity to meet and study with many of the most respected mediums in the world--John Holland, Tim Braun, James Van Praagh, to name a few. When Teresa Caputo, the Long Island Medium, filled an auditorium, Sylvia won the opportunity to go backstage and meet her in person.

I've watched Sylvia grow from being occasionally intuitive to being a reliable medium. She's accomplished this through study and effort. She joined a spiritual development circle that emphasized mediumship. Experiencing the sudden death of her friend served as a catalyst for a whole new area of personal development.

She invited me to several events that dispelled many of my religious fear-based reservations. There can be great value in reaching beyond the veil to nonphysical loved ones. Death often comes violently, painfully, or unexpectedly, leaving family members emotionally wounded. Guilt or anger can linger a lifetime. God gets blamed. Faith is lost.

Tim Braun

Mediums can serve as healing conduits between separated loved ones. Sylvia took me to a Tim Braun presentation. He is an engaging, likable young man. Spirit communication began for him at the age of seven. He's done over 14,000 readings. Some of the evening was fun and entertaining, like the bossy, Italian grandmother coming through to her several daughters in the audience. Some messages were heart breaking, especially the young man who had committed suicide.

Spirit Communication is Tim's life work. With such a strong talent, what else could he do? Why does he do it? From his website:

It is Tim's desire to heal those with grief of loss, and to re-establish the ties that we have lost with those no longer with us. Tim believes our love is the link that allows us to connect with those on the other side. Many of Tim's clients have had their lives changed dramatically, and have been given hope that there is a place of beauty and joy that exists at the end of our lives on earth. Loved ones are there, and love doesn't die, but is taken to this place called "the other side."

The Children Speak

Losing a child is probably the deepest grief. Our worst fear. Never-ending pain. It seems so WRONG. Medium

Maureen Hancock offers parents the opportunity to know their child is still a vital spirit. Here is a message she relays in her book, *The Medium Next Door:*

Tell my parents I am okay. When I came over, everyone stood in a circle to greet me. I felt like I was wrapped in a warm blanket, and I knew everything would be all right. I was filled with love. There is no real time in heaven, and I take comfort in knowing I will see my parents and siblings again. I was the first to take the path, but I won't be the last. Tell them my love for them will never die. Tell them to smile and laugh for me--and not feel guilty about it--because it fills my spirit with such joy to know they are living for me. I am living through them. I will make my presence known to them...a song on the radio, a coin with the date of my birth, a beautiful bird that catches their eye, my jersey number, a call with nobody on the line, and best of all, a dream where I hug or tell them, "I'm not dead. I'm just different."

The Thinning Veil

It appears to me that spirit communication is part of the New Normal. My theory is it related to the earth moving into the new cosmic age that began in 1987 with the harmonic conversion and was completed in December of 2012. Information about The Shift is readily available. Gregg Braden wrote extensively on the subject. Kryon has many channelings of information. He also talks about "time capsules" opening that have released higher frequencies on the planet.

Whatever the explanation, something is happening. Something has changed. Formerly "ordinary" people are having visions, hearing voices, communicating with animals or nonphysical beings. They question their sanity. They don't tell anyone for fear of ridicule.

Time to examine whether fears are rational or old programming from an outdated paradigm. Certainly common sense, discernment, and a healthy dose of skepticism are recommended to judge each experience. Each spirit communicator is a unique individual. Some are more skilled than others. Some are more ethical than others. As with everything in life, buyer beware. But, don't avoid a positive experience, perhaps soul-healing opportunity because of fear. Do not let fear defeat you.

My Husband's Messages

My husband, David, died in a one car accident in February 2013. Immediately after his passing, I received a variety of indications he was very much alive in spirit. I found dimes around the house--on the floor, on counters and shelves. Once during a somewhat unflattering conversation about him in my daughter's kitchen, the light over the table dimmed dramatically. We changed the subject.

I went to Sylvia's spiritual development circle, as their "test" subject. They didn't know me or my past. He came through, loud and clear.

One said, "I see a man showing me happy times, perhaps in the 80's. Fishing and family vacations. He liked those the best. He loved his family, but didn't always show it."

Another said, "I see a man pushing everyone out of the way. He's showing me legal papers. He's saying they are signed."

That one made me blink for sure. David was a lawyer. He had prepared his mother's will, but we never found signed copies. I guess we just didn't know where to look!

I asked if he was pleased with the way I had disposed of his theological books. The reader said, "He's giving me the thumbs up sign." His books had been his most dear possessions. I hated the thought of dumping them off at a used book store where few would appreciate them. I ran a Craigslist ad. A pastor and his son picked them up for their church library. They were happy. I was happy. I was glad to find out David was happy.

So far, I haven't displayed great mediumship talent. Of course, I haven't pursued it. Seeing the progress Sylvia made through her exercises, I suspect it's a multidimensional skill that can be developed.

There have been times I've had "witching hour" encounters. Supposedly around 4am, the frequencies are such just before sunrise that spirits can communicate easier with the 3-D earth plane.

I'll close this segment on spirit communication with my emotional final "goodbye" to David that happened before dawn a few months after he passed. It was one of the most moving, bittersweet experiences of my life.

Here's the post I wrote at Supernal Living in July of 2013:

David and Dana, 1992

It's been six months since my husband was suddenly gone in a car accident last February. Only six months, yet, a lifetime. The surreal first month, caught in a flurry of details and rituals. The memorial service panorama of faces across a thirty-six year marriage passing before me in one afternoon.... Carrying a box of ashes to a droughty cemetery in Norman, Oklahoma. Leaving them on the desk of a friendly, Okie-speak girl for later burial in his parents' plot.

I kept waiting to see my phone ringing showing "husband" and I'd tell him all about it.

The weeks back home in California melted into tasks accomplished-- sending death certificates, a new trust drawn up, closets cleaned, home repairs. Long, quiet nights.

Emotion held at bay until a witching hour visit last month. Supposedly between 4 and 5 o'clock in the morning our spirit selves can make contact with the other side. There have been similar "dreams" where I'm lying in my bed, asleep and yet aware. I can see and hear a normally unseen dimension around me. One night I heard a grand party going on and a man stood next to my bed playing a saxophone. As I awakened to complete consciousness, he disappeared; the music faded. Last January my dear friend, Jeanie, appeared a week after she'd passed over. Her grandson sat on the foot of my bed as she spoke lovingly to me to say goodbye.

The visitation/dream from my husband, David, came five months after he got confused driving in road construction along I-35, hit a cone, spun into a concrete wall and was then broadsided by a van.

As I lay in my bed, dawn was an hour away, when I was awakened by the sound of running water. David stood next to the window, his back to me, wearing only his boxers, which was always his sleeping attire. He seemed to be washing his hands, another nighttime ritual. My first thought was, "There's no sink there." (Our Oklahoma bedroom had a sink outside the shower. In my California home, the bathroom is down the hall.)

He looked at me over his shoulder and smiled. I got the impression he could do special things in this spirit dimension, even conjure up a sink. He stepped to the bed and slipped between the covers with me. After months of solitary sleeping, the intense joy of feeling my husband next me was beyond description. Our arms joined like, two halves of whole fitting together.

His face was bathed in a golden glow. He looked 35 again. The handsome guy I married. "You look good," I said.

"So do you," he said. He pulled me closer. "I was so stupid. I crawled away. I wrecked the car."

An image played in my mind of his spirit body seeing the aftermath of his accident, the chaos and destruction. He watched helplessly, irritated with himself for making an irrevocable error of judgment.

Until that moment, I'd pictured him going to the light, surrounded by angels walking into a pink sunset. A Hollywood ending. Maybe that came later.

In our bed, I felt the regret and the longing and the last goodbye. He stretched out over me. So wonderful, so right, so fleeting. My arms gathered across his back and held on as long as it would last. I knew it wasn't real and yet it was utterly real.

Don't go...don't go....

As the rays of sunlight rose above the horizon, he dissolved in my arms. I came to full consciousness, flat on my back, tears trailing into my hair. I lay there two more hours, flummoxed, gob-smacked.

A true period of grief began. Sadness, weeping spells. Also, came the grace. A prophetic friend living hundreds of miles away sent me a "word from the Lord." My pain was not unnoticed.... A wonderful healer gave me a full body massage and therapy session... I took a class in sound therapy and received a whole array of healing frequencies from bells, singing bowls, tuning forks and Reiki.... My Supernal friend, Sue, administered a healing energy treatment to heal regret.

After thirty-six years, there were regrets. I was focusing on the lost opportunities and missed moments. The healers helped me turn from regret, move toward gratitude and remember the happy times. I needed to be grateful for the family we created--first, two fabulous daughters and now two wonderful grand kids and the joyful anticipation of the next one in February. Yes, a year from David's departure, we will be welcoming our younger daughter's first child into our lives.

It seems only appropriate to end this with a passage from the Bible, the book that held my husband's constant fascination and guided his life.

Thou hast turned for me my mourning into dancing; thou hast loosed my sackcloth and girded me with gladness Psalms 30:11

Chapter Seven ~ Channeling

Supernal Journals ~ February 23, 2011

Meeting at Dana's house. Sue came in with a sore back. We began our meditation time. I spoke out loud and invited angels and spiritual companions to join us. I asked the Holy Spirit to join us and guide us. We were quiet many minutes. Paula slipped into an unconscious state. Sue began to hear phrases:

"Come from strength"

"The hour of weakness is passed"

"Gird your loins"

She looked at me with a sheepish expression and said, "Don't laugh." I assured her I wouldn't. She said, "I heard 'Look for amber eyes.'"

I shook my head. That made no sense to me. "Look for amber eyes?"

Then Paula roused and said, "What is this strange food?"

She pulled something out of her mouth and held it between her thumb and index finger. "It's sticky."

It was gum. I walked across the room and took it from her and threw it into the kitchen trash as I explained, "It's gum. It comes from a tree."

Clearly, we were no longer talking to Paula. Sue and I exchanged looks. I ran to get my notebook.

I asked, "Have we ever talked before?"

"No."

"What is your name?"

"Amberayse."

Sue and I shared another electric glance. She had gotten the words a little off--"amber eyes" is the name of an entity--Amberayse-- coming through Paula.

Paula spoke easily and opened her eyes. She looked all over the room, obviously seeing things invisible to Sue and me.

She said, "The room is filled with spirits. A large angel hovers behind you." (Dana)

My dad and their father were also in the room. She said we all work together and see each other in classes. (in another dimension? when we sleep?)

She admonished us to stay together and not disband. (Sue had been thinking of leaving the group because she couldn't sense any particular psychic talent. She just "heard things.")

Amberayse said when we get together we bring a higher vibration that has a ripple effect and brings healing to the planet. People receive healing vibrations from our meditation times. We are supposed to meet more frequently and set a time to pray even when we're not together.

Sue's back was better after the session.

The New Normal

Before our Supernal Friends sessions, channeling seemed like the stuff of gypsies, gurus, mystics, or other various weird people. Nothing "normal" people like my lifelong friends would ever exhibit. Not us motherly, career gal, middle class Americans.

Well, welcome to the New Normal.

Sue, Paula, and I had each embarked on our personal explorations of multidimensional living and came together as time and circumstances allowed. Together, our energy seemed to unite and create something stronger than the sum of its parts.

The crowns of our heads felt wide open. The pineal gland is credited with being the opening to spiritual energy. I can attest to a very real physical sensation of expansion, warmth, and "buzzing."

Paula, the one who had suffered the most from a lifetime of ailments, also displayed the strongest psychic gifts. During our meditations, Paula began "falling asleep," inadvertently opening her mind and body for other worldly visitors. A few times she transformed with a very strong, male energy. Both Sue and I got the impression of an Indian shaman. Paula didn't say anything, but performed intricate symbols with her hands. We asked questions, but received no answers. About the third time, I had my camera ready and filmed it.

Once Paula came back to herself and saw the video she didn't like what she saw at all. She felt invaded. Later, in her meditations at home she told Mr. Medicine Man to move on.

Other channelings, like the sessions with Amberayse were more welcome and productive. Generally, our spiritual visitors encouraged us to keep up our healing work. The sessions might have been more productive if Sue and I had been better moderators and come up with meaningful questions.

Also, Paula was a somewhat reluctant channeler. She never got comfortable thinking she had simply awakened from a nap, to find us staring at her in wide-eyed wonder.

"What happened?"

"It was so amazing. You marched across the room with your eyes closed and gave us attunements. You don't remember?"

Paula prefers staying conscious. Becoming a full-time channeler isn't her ambition. She experienced it in the safe environment of our Supernal Friends sessions, but she isn't taking it on the road.

Yet, those sessions were an important expansion of our spiritual understanding. The three of us realized "regular" people could tap into multiple realms of consciousness.

Channeling went from weird to wonderful; from odd to normal.

What is Channeling?

A person is able to open a dimension of information and become a "spirit communicator." The thoughts and ideas of the nonphysical being transmit through the human being. This ability is more common than recognized. You don't have to be completely taken over by your dead Aunt Nelly or some other entity to be an effective channel. Artists, writers, musicians, inventors, and trend setters innately open their creative abilities to inspiration from beyond the veil.

The composer Handel reported seeing angels during the three weeks he was secluded writing *The Messiah*. The rediscovered genius of invention, Nikola Tesla, was surely a channel. His inventions changed our entire way of living. He gave us modern light and sound technology. Electricity, radio waves, the electric motor, lasers, wireless communication-it can all be traced to the inspirations and inventions of Nikola Tesla.

Nikola Tesla ~ "There is some core in space where we get all the strength, all the inspiration, what attracts us eternally, I feel its power and value which is emitted to the whole space and keeps it in harmony. I didn't discover the secret, but know that exists."

Where the line between inspiration begins and channeling begins is fuzzy. Artists often wait until their inspiration comes from "out there." They hear the tune...see the image...get the idea.

Fear Factor

Of course, pure channeling involves the certainty that other entities are involved. That's when it can get a little scary.

Terms like "channeling" and "mediumship" carry Christian phobia baggage. Fear of evil and demonic possession is deep seated in our society. However, change the name and it's okay. If someone is declared a "prophet" getting "words of knowledge," many Christian groups embrace such information as Divine Inspiration. Religions and cults of all flavors generally credit some prophet with getting instructions straight from God.

Channeling by any other name....

I'm sure psychologists, psychiatrists, and other PHD-types would simply label it mental illness and delusional behavior.

Think for Yourself

Is it real? Is it fake? Is it from God? Is it from ET's? Is it from evil entities? Is it from angels? Is it imagination? Maybe...to all of the above.

If some channeled material seems intriguing, check it out. Decide for yourself whether it resonants with truth or is pure bunk. Having seen channeling in action through Paula, I believe that channeling can happen. Paula was the real deal. I have no doubt about that. Somehow, the personality of my friend was able to also transmit information from another nonphysical presence. That's about all I know for sure.

Paula did not choose to become a full time communicator for any certain entity. She is working in other directions. Watching her, my mind opened to exploring channeled material out of pure curiosity. But that doesn't mean I left my common sense, intelligence, or intuition at the curb.

From the Ridiculous to the Sublime

Nowadays a Google search on channeled messages will yield a cornucopia of oracles, angels, and ascended masters finding their human mouthpieces to transmit their wisdom to mankind. The Archangel Michael and St. Germain appear to have many contacts. YouTube is another treasure trove of audio and video channeling experiences. Some are very doomsday; others are all esoteric gobbledegook. Among the floating debris are fascinating ideas about spirituality, quantum realities, and expanding human consciousness.

Modern Mystics

One of the most interesting and notable channelers of the 20th century was Edgar Cayce (1877-1945), dubbed *The Sleeping Prophet* in the 1960's biography authored by Jess Stern. Born in a small Kentucky town, Cayce appeared to be the most unlikely of mystics. Seemingly a simple country fellow with a deep Christian faith, he supported his young family as a photographer in the early 1900's. Yet, when he "fell asleep," he had the ability to diagnose and prescribe for patients long distance. Edgar Cayce didn't channel another entity, but rather his Higher Self. Over the course of forty years, the carefully recorded readings and files maintained by his secretary and family provide a wealth of alternative health remedies, future predictions, and esoteric material. Through many ups and downs of fortune, Cayce and his devoted followers laid the groundwork for much of the metaphysical and natural health movements popular today. Cayce's story has been the fodder for countless books. Hopefully, someday someone will produce a definitive film about his work and life. His foundation, the A.R.E. (Association for Research and Enlightenment) is still going strong in Virginia Beach, Virginia. Visit EdgarCayce.org for more information.

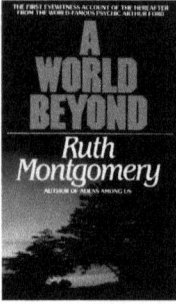

Popular channelers who developed celebrity status in the latter part of the 20th century included Ruth Montgomery (1912-2001), and JZ Knight (Ramtha) (1946--). Montgomery employed her reporter's writing skills to produce a series of bestselling books via channeled automatic writing material from a group entity called "Lily." Later, her friend, Arthur Ford, came through after his death. Montgomery's predictions caught the public's attention, even if they often fizzled under the scrutiny of time. Her interest in reincarnation creaked open the closed door of Western thinking on that subject. Her books have largely faded from the spotlight.

JZ Knight has been channeling a 35,000 year old entity, Ramtha from Lemuria, since the 1970's. Ramtha's persona completely overtakes Knight's body in speech patterns and mannerisms. Frankly, the Ramtha material has not personally resonated with me. However, she is still going strong in the Mt. Ranier, Washington area. She runs a school, offers courses in energy healing, presents many global predictions, and has faithful followers. She was featured in the popular quantum physics film *What The Bleep Do We Know*. If you're intrigued, find more information at JZKnight.com.

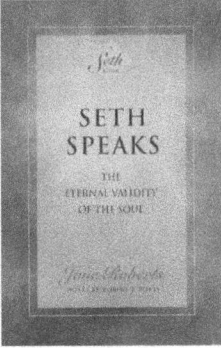

My earliest exposure to channeled material were the Seth books by Jane Roberts in the 1970's. I read them covertly while residing in the Bible Belt. I certainly couldn't have discussed them at church potlucks. They launched the New Age Movement. From 1963 until her death in 1984, Jane Roberts trance channeled esoteric material expounding ideas that later led to catch phrases like "change your thinking, change your life" and "everyone creates their own reality" and certainly paved the way for "The Law of Attraction." The Seth material is still available and curated by The Seth Learning Center.

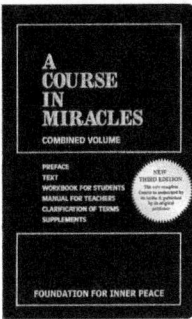

About the same time the Seth material was coming through to Jane Roberts, a clinical psychologist who taught at Columbia University named Helen Schucman began scribing a channeled tome that begins, *this is a course in miracles*. Schucman worked over the span of seven years writing out in short hand the verbiage coming through her mind. She handed the material as it unfolded to a colleague, William Thetford, who typed and organized it. The otherworldly author of the material eventually identified himself as Jesus, though *A Course in Miracles* is not to be construed as a third testament continuation of the Bible. It is a course of self-study to ultimately transform the world view of the student. It bears common threads to the New Testament with allusions to the Holy Spirit and references to the Crucifixion and the Resurrection. The theme of Forgiveness is paramount, both of others and oneself. It departs from accepted Christian theology over issues like eternal damnation and separation from God.

A Course in Miracles is a unique manuscript, now fifty years old, and gaining students around the globe. The Foundation of Inner Peace at ACIM.org. has overseen the translation of ACIM into twenty-three languages, so far.

Schucman's identity as "scribe" of the material was withheld until after her death in 1981. I can only begin to imagine what it must have been like to have the words coming through her mind. She surely must have wondered about her sanity at times.

At any rate, *A Course in Miracles* is purely channeled material. It is not easy or quick reading. It took me a year to work through it. I'm sure there is much I did not grasp. But, I think it made me a stronger, calmer person. There is an analogy that always comes to mind of myself before and after ACIM--I was like a dull glass pitcher, full of little cracks, leaky, liable to break apart at any moment. After ACIM, I am a clear glass, unbroken pitcher, able to hold my own, quietly ready to do my job, whatever it might be.

A Course in Miracles is still in its earliest, and probably purest, era. It will be interesting to see if new leadership will continue in the low-key manner of their predecessors, or if egos will battle for control and notoriety as the years go by. I hope it can stay a philosophy rather than morphing into a new religion.

Jesus Speaks, Again

Canadian Tina Louise Spalding began channeling Jesus in 2014, at least that's the claim. She has been channeling a soul group called Ananda since 2012. She has quietly published *Jesus, My Autobiography.* Am I convinced it's the real deal? Well, Jesus has not personally contacted me to verify his authorship. However, I found the material very intriguing. In an earlier era Ms. Spalding would have certainly been killed for blasphemy, heresy, and sorcery. I would have likewise met some hateful, grisly demise for simply reading the book. Fortunately, we live in more freethinking times. From the Preface:

I talk about the truth of my birth and the truth of my life. I cover some stories that are recounted in the Bible and tell you the true story of those events. I describe my personal traits, my human traits, and I define what I am, who I am, and why these things happened. You will be able to understand the truth, and you will begin this reconditioning, this retooling of your mind -- of your thoughts and beliefs -- on this subject of my life, my meaning, and my purpose, for it is a long process. The time is ripe. The need for a spiritual revolution is here. -- Jesus

Written in the first person, Jesus covers his childhood and his travels from ages fourteen to thirty-three not mentioned in the Bible. Whether "true" or not, Jesus becomes a very human person: a curious boy, a dissatisfied youth, a seeker of adventure and spiritual enlightenment. He reveals his great love and subsequent marriage to Mary Magdalene. He comes across as a very spiritually evolved man with a message of Love that didn't change the world nearly as much as he'd hoped it would. He challenges the established church and states much of the Bible was twisted to promote a political agenda. (He's not the first to make that claim.)

Mainstream Christian believers will be utterly uncomfortable with this Jesus, who denies his unique Divinity as the only Son of God. However, millennia of worshipers has had its effect:

Chapter Fifteen excerpt: *There are many people who have offered up their lives as sacrifices to me, and what I say is this: The focus of human consciousness on one being shifts that being's consciousness. Because I have had such adoration and love from so many -- the prayers and focused consciousness of so many millions of people over such a long time have indeed shifted my consciousness far beyond that which I could have done by myself. So you can see that the inadvertent belief in my divinity has caused that very thing to arise in some ways.*

I have become so enlivened by these wonderful prayers. I have become so connected to so many humans through their willingness to speak to me. I have been given a lot of responsibility in the nonphysical to offer truth out to beings who speak to me, commune with me on a consciousness level, and try to meld with me in prayer.

The details of his earthly existence over two thousand years ago are not the main meat of the manuscript. The most inspirational parts speak to modern spiritual seekers. He covers many subjects including:

- The Spiritual Mind vs the Ego Mind
- Manifesting Health
- Change Your Mind to Transform the World
- Forgiving Yourself
- Sexual Energy
- A New Paradigm
- Passion and Purpose

Jesus, My Autobiography feels very much like a companion piece to *A Course in Miracles.* He claims authorship of ACIM and recommends people read it. The message of forgiveness, love, and compassion is the same. Whether the book is authentic or fictionalized, it presents a wise, spiritually advanced Jesus who is far more appealing than the judgmental Jesus often portrayed in religious groups. It's certainly a fresh look at Jesus, the man, and is chocked full of wise advice for modern times.

Jesus Calling

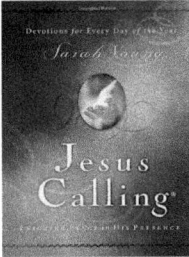

Christian author, Sarah Young, and her publisher Thomas Nelson, might take issue with being included in this mix of metaphysical authors, but it's my opinion that the bestselling book, *Jesus Calling*, has all the earmarks of being channeled material. In the Preface, Young reveals being aware of a Presence and identifies it as Jesus. She later changes her journaling from a diary to a listening process.

I wanted to hear what God had to say to me personally on a given day. I decided to listen to God with pen in hand, writing down whatever I believed He was saying.

Jesus Calling evolved into a daily devotional, cross-referenced with Biblical scripture to validate the messages. The daily messages are uplifting and personal. They portray an interactive loving, spiritual Presence that is popular with millions of readers.

Its huge success has spawned a whole genre of *Jesus Calling* books. Whether you label it "channeled" or "inspired," *Jesus Calling* continues to be at the top of the bestseller charts.

Entities from Beyond

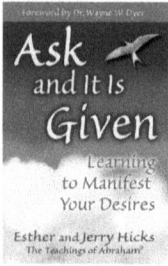

In 1985 an attractive "normal" American woman named Esther Hicks began channeling a group of nonphysical teachers collectively called Abraham. Esther's husband, Jerry, proved to be the perfect partner for communicating with Abraham while Esther's persona rested on an etherial bench. Jerry's enthusiasm for esoteric conversations and Esther's ability to step aside and let the thoughts flow opened a floodgate of information. Jerry's marketing skills catapulted Abraham-Hicks into spirituality superstars status, best known for leading the Law of Attraction vanguard.

Esther Hicks

During a time when I was struggling being the caretaker for my father after his stroke in 2003, Sue loaned me a set of Abraham CD's to listen to as I walked around my hometown neighborhood. As I pounded the pavement to work off tension, Esther's slightly accented Abraham voice began feeding me life-changing concepts about the law of attraction. At that time, my life seemed like one big struggle--financial, physical, emotional. You name it. I was just hanging on, fighting the good fight.

Suddenly I began to wonder--how were my actions, my thoughts, my beliefs creating the very struggles I kept facing? I'd thought all these things "just happened." Or perhaps were God's challenges or bad karma or simply rotten luck. The Abraham material began turning on my lights. Was I somehow attracting the very things I disliked? Was I living at an energetic level of disharmony? My vocabulary expanded with words like "frequency," "vibrations," and "vortex."

Maybe I was getting a little "weird," but I was also getting balanced, more observant of human behavior, and beginning to comprehend the power of intention.

Though Jerry Hicks passed "into the nonphysical" in November of 2011, Esther is continuing the work they began, writing books, touring with Deepak Chopra and continuing to share the Abraham messages with audiences across the world.

Learn more about Esther and Abraham at Abraham-Hicks.com

Beyond the Law of Attraction

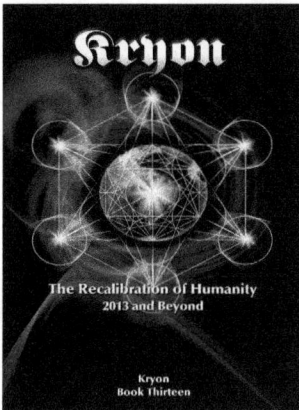

Lee Carroll began sharing the channeled messages he was receiving from a "loving angelic entity" called Kryon in 1989. Lee also seems like a "normal" guy. After earning a business and economics degree, he ran a technical audio business for thirty years in San Diego. The Kryon experience "hit him between the eyes."

Carroll revealed the first messages to small metaphysical groups in Southern California. Through the years a "Kryon Team" has assembled to present seminars around the world. He has spoken to the

United Nations in New York City on seven occasions. His audiences have filled auditoriums, churches, and meeting halls around the world. Visit the Kryon.com Memorable Seminars page. The Lee Carroll/Kryon messages culminate the seminars. Lee sits with his eyes closed, "steps aside," and allows Kryon to speak through him. Messages are generally forty-five minutes or less.

Through the years, Carroll has compiled a series of books assembling the messages regarding various subjects. Recently he has authorized other writers to assemble books incorporating Kryon channelings.

While the Abraham-Hicks material has reiterated the law of attraction again and again, the Kryon messages have taken a more evolutionary route. Kryon speaks to the "old souls," the one-half-of-one percent of the population that will "get" what he's talking about. As a teacher he had to begin with his kindergarten class, so to speak. The earliest Kryon books relate parables, resembling children's stories, yet laden with esoteric symbolism. The lessons of the stories are carefully explained by Carroll as he edited the books, lest anyone not understand the morals of the stories.

Through the years, Kryon and Carroll have perfected their "partnership," while opening up broader and broader esoteric subjects. God, angels, death, human development, creation of the universe, earth energy, extraterrestrials, Atlantis, Lumeria, reincarnation, quantum physics, DNA--you name it, Kryon has probably talked about it. He reminds me of an ET Socrates, expounding philosophy and forcing his students to question all their beliefs.

I enjoy reading and listening to Kryon. He picked a strong voice with Carroll. Each message begins: "I am Kryon of Magnetic Service. My partner steps aside...." His delivery style ranges from gentle teaching to enthusiastic sermonizing. He often ends with "I am Kryon. In love with humanity. And so it is."

The overriding arc of Kryon's messages is preparing humanity for the New Age, a term which by now is laden with about a million pounds of baggage. Nevertheless, he often refers to a timeline that has been unfolding over the past decades. There was the harmonic convergence of 1987 heading into The Shift made famous by the December 21, 2012 Mayan calendar hoopla. Kryon and others maintain the earth has moved into a new galactic era as we spin around the Milky Way. The energies and frequencies are shifting, affecting all life on planet earth. He has arrived as a nonphysical teacher to help us understand the impact and implications of these changes.

People are transforming. Indeed, our offspring are different than previous generations. Lee Carroll and a collaborator, Jan Tabor, were the first to identify the Indigo Children, so named because of unique purplish hue in their auric fields. There have been "Indigos" throughout history. Now, they are incarnating in record numbers. These children are wired differently; they are gifted, but often don't assimilate easily into social situations. Many children being labeled autistic and ADHD are these new-model humans. They think, feel, and act differently than previous generations. At their best, with guidance and nurturing, they're bringing innovations to every field of human endeavor.

In the final analysis, Kryon delivers messages of hope for the human race. We aren't going to destroy the earth; we're capable of creative solutions for every stupid destructive policy from the "old energy." We can leave "survival mode" and move into an era of peace and plenty. We are rising to a higher level of consciousness, kindness, and generosity.

I hope he's right.

Visit Kryon.com and explore the many free recordings of the past decades. Pick out a book on a subject that captures your interest. Kryon is quite a fascinating fellow.

Evolution of a Channeler

Thanks to the Internet, I've become cyberfriends with spiritually mindful people around the world. Many of them reside in Australia. I've had the good fortune to discover healer and channeler, Janice Hunneybell. She has published two books of channeled material from the unlikely source of the American singer, John Denver. *Things That I Believe In* and *All You Need is Love* are delightful, filled with inspirational insights written with a strong John Denver voice, especially the first book.

Janice Hunneybell

I interviewed Jan via Skype to gain better insight into how her channeling talents evolved. Jan was born in post-World War II England. While she didn't have the happiest of childhoods, she didn't have the worst. She married and had children. She was "normal."

Of course, like many of us, "normal" had its ups and downs. She enjoyed a fair amount of "woman's intuition," but wouldn't have put herself in a psychic category. Moving to Australia with her husband and children in 1989 sent her into an emotional tailspin. She missed England and struggled to find her footing in her new home. After wallowing in despair for several months, one day she was thinking about how unhappy she was when she heard a male voice in her mind, asking, *Are you going to be miserable for the rest of your life or are you going to do something about it?*

This was a new experience but she somehow knew this 'voice' cared and was challenging her to think differently, so she made a choice for change. Jan returned to study and later joined groups at a local healing center.

One early morning in 1996 she awoke at 4:30 and heard a voice say, *you can heal with these hands*. Reiki soon came into her life – she didn't know what it was, but knew she had to do it. After receiving treatments, she signed up for a Reiki I class and received the level one attunement.

Jan recalled, "During the night after the Reiki I attunement I woke and had the sense of being surrounded by many people, including one bigger, more powerful being. I felt a surge of energy and went back to sleep. When I woke again I wondered what had happened to me and heard the words 'integration of self.' A few days later, in meditation, I felt myself growing, a little like Alice in Wonderland. I expanded into the clouds, yet felt the earth was still beneath my feet. I was surrounded by guides and angels. Jesus was there, which surprised me because I wasn't a follower, although I believed in him. He spoke with me and at the end, two angels, one pink and one blue, stood on either side of me. They shrank before my eyes and went into my ears! I heard them say, *we are with you always."*

She became clairaudient. Poems poured into her mind. She worked with healing energy, studied healing modalities, attended classes, and followed her Higher Self inner wisdom. By 1997 she felt she needed to open herself to channeling.

She received an energy treatment from her Reiki Master. "I felt like I was going through a birth canal," she said.

During an afternoon with her spiritual teacher, her first guide, Arthur, came through. He helped her calm the chatter of mind talk to be an effective channel. Arthur exemplified unconditional love. He shared his philosophy and became a treasured teacher. Later, on a trip to England she visited Glastonbury, the ancient home and burial grounds of the fabled King Arthur and Queen Guinevere. Walking the gardens she became overwhelmed with emotion and heard, *I am Arthur, son of Uther Pendragon.* Was her guide, Arthur, the spirit of the Arthurian legends?

Jan smiles wistfully, "It can't be proven, but I like to think so."

At any rate, the door to channeling opened in her mind. She received messages from many nonphysical beings, including some historical figures such as Mother Mary and St. Francis. In September of that year a medium told her to expect an American connection and she saw a crashed biplane.

JD Speaks

On Sunday the 12th of October 1997 John Denver died when his two-seater plane crashed into the ocean off the coast of California. It was Monday the 13th in Australia. Six days later, Jan felt a spike of emotion, a huge smile spread across her face and she heard, *good afternoon, it's lovely to be here*. John Denver became a regular visitor, often giving her beautiful lyrics to songs.

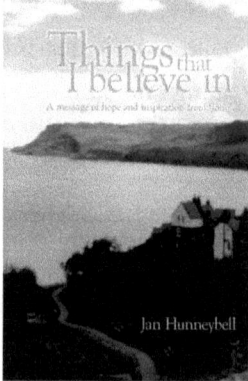

By September of 2001, she knew she would be writing a book, but didn't know what it would be. She had grown in her ability to focus and channel for significant periods of time. She agreed to devote two hours a day to the project. JD began to dictate. The book came through over the course of one month, with very little editing needed. *Things That I Believe In* communicated the words and wisdom of John Denver, a passionate man who loved music, life, and the planet. Even in the nonphysical state, he still wanted to make a positive impact on the world. The book's description says:

Through the mediumship of Janice Hunneybell, John, a singer, songwriter and environmentalist, communicates from beyond with the message that human consciousness continues after physical death. He

*shares his thoughts on life's deepest questions - what happens when we
die and why we are here - and talks about forgiveness, gratitude, fear
and many other subjects in an informal but informative way, illustrating
his message with personal examples. With the wisdom of hindsight,
having looked back on the lessons of his own life and also having
learned a great deal since his dramatic exit from the physical world,
John gives his opinion on how to make the most of the life we have.*

Getting the book from a raw manuscript to publication was a learning journey. Much like *A Course In Miracles* that began merely being copied on copy machines and passed around, *Things That I Believe In* was first read by members of the Spiritualist Church in Melbourne in a similar manner. People began encouraging Jan to have it published and available to the mass market. With the rise of digital publishing, both books of JD's words of wisdom and love are finding a global audience.

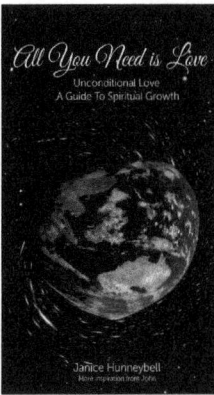

All You Need is Love came through later with more pure information and less of the John Denver personality. When asked why much of the information came as voiceless words rather than in John's voice, Spirit told her it took less energy to transmit the information that way. When she re-read the manuscript, John's presence and voice was with her once more, adding additional insights as she reviewed what had been written – and reassuring her that these were his words.

Both books offer inspiration and encouragement from beyond the veil for people to make the most of their time on earth.

Jan continues her spiritual journey. JD appears to have moved on, but she has a growing healing and mediumship practice. Visit her Facebook site *Janice Hunneybell -- Inspired Thoughts* to glimpse inside the mind of a gifted medium channel.

Personal Channeling

Can a "normal," mildly intuitive person, such as myself be an effective channeler? And why would I want to do that anyway? Channeling simply as a party game, like playing a Ouija board, holds no interest for me. Nor do I care to be the human voice for an angel, ET, or ascended master. However, getting in better communication with my "team," the spiritual helpers I sense, but cannot see, does appeal to me.

Getting more in touch with wisdom seems worth the effort. The Higher Self is frequently mentioned in metaphysical material. Higher Self is the notion that only a portion of our souls incarnate into the physical plane. The other portion--the Higher Self--remains on the other side of the veil, though always connected with the human. There might even be another incarnation with a portion of the same soul leading a different life at the same time. *Stop, that is too mind-blowing.* I can only handle the idea of one me on the planet at a time.

Most of us sense there is much more to us than we understand. Since Freud, we've accepted the psychological explanation of conscious and subconscious. Hypnotherapy opens up hidden memories and even past lives. Dr. Michael Newton's hypnosis patients revealed their lives *between* lives.

Meditation opens the communication channels to Higher Self information. I want to live a happy, productive life. The first step is getting in touch every morning with Myself and any helpers I may have. Keeping a notebook nearby is essential to capture ideas drifting by.

Out of the Blue

Occasionally, I'll write something down and look back thinking surely someone else was coming through.

Supernal Journals ~ July 20, 2014

The oceans cleanse the earth. The turbulence is a washing cycle. Light beams from the universe into the ocean. An exchange of energy occurs. This is the way the earth is "charged" with the force that sustains life. Do not fear the storms. They are part of the cycle.

I have no memory of writing that down. Maybe I was praying about a hurricane. Are the ideas expressed valid? Beats me. That passage is completely "out of the blue." Often my prayer and mediation sessions include sending healing energy to the ocean.

Here's a message that offered insights on sacred geometry that I'd never thought of before. Truthfully, I hadn't even put "sacred" together with "geometry." After the message I went on-line to learn more.

Supernal Journals ~ June 22, 2013

We will teach you of sacred geometry. The symbols act as connections between one dimension and the next. They each have a unique frequency that is absorbed by the person who receives them through the attunement process.

The symbols can also be embedded in books, music, plants, and objects. The ancient people knew this and carved them in stone to raise the vibrations of their communities. We will give you sacred geometry as you work as a therapist to bring clarity and raise the frequency of your clients. That is all.

That message raised my awareness and understanding of the Reiki symbols and other attunement symbols. Every spontaneous attunement Sue and I ever received from Paula always included symbols she traced on our palms and foreheads. I get the impression the symbols are absorbed in our auric fields, adding frequencies, like new notes on a piano.

Channeling is the communication stream between people and spirit. Think of a radio. Meditation turns it on. Channeling finds the station. There are many stations. Higher Self. Holy Spirit. Angels. The departed. ET's. If you don't like the channel, change it. You are always in control of the dial and the power switch.

Fear based theologies and superstitions keep people turned off, afraid the devil or evil spirits will invade them. Biblical advice comes from James 4:7 *Resist the devil and he will flee from you.*

Set an intention of seeking higher entities such as God, angels, and the Holy Spirit for loving, helpful encounters. Channeling then serves as the communication method.

Take notes. Spirit has much to share, if you are willing to listen.

Chapter Eight ~

Pre-Life Planning and Exit Points

Supernal Journals ~ September 20, 2006

Sue was very ill last week with a flu. I called her to check up on her. She said she was napping on the couch a lot. She sounded very weak, but said she was taking care of herself and turned down offers of help. She didn't want anyone else to get ill, so Paula and I just kept calling.

On the third day in, she didn't sound much better. She said, "I just had the strangest dream."

"Oh, yeah, what was it?"

"I was driving on a freeway. I drove past Exit 52. I kept driving and then I passed another sign and it also said Exit 52. I drove and kept passing Exit 52. Isn't that strange?" she said weakly.

Oh my gosh. Exit 52! Though Sue was too sick to remember or understand the message of the dream, I knew exactly what it meant. Last year Sue had an Akashic Records reading with Helen and asked about her exit points. Helen could see several exit points.

"I see ones at 19 and 28." Sue recalled her car wreck at 17 and the emergency C-section at 28. In another era, she and her baby would have died.

"I see one at 52. Are you 53 now?" Helen had asked.

"I'm 51." Hmmm.

Sue is now 52. Exit 52! She is sicker than she knows.

Paula and I alerted Sue's adult children about the severity of her illness. Her son and daughter ignored her protestations of being a bother. Her son bought medications and hydrating drinks. Her daughter moved in for a couple of days and took charge of nursing. Indeed, Sue was running high fevers and even hallucinating for a while. Without intervention, she could have gotten deathly ill.

We thanked Spirit for giving us the information through Helen and dreams before she got on the offramp of Exit 52.

My first exposure to Exit Points popped up during Akashic Records readings from Helen. Evidently, there is quite a system of pre-life planning we humans make before incarnating, which was news to me.

My American Christian culture had taught me a baby is a blank palette, influenced by genetics and nurturing (nature vs. nurture). The baby grows into adulthood and then dies, at some pre-appointed time. (*When your number is up, your number is up.*) The person either goes to heaven or hell, depending upon whether Jesus Christ was accepted as Lord and Savior somewhere along the way. So begins eternity. No do-overs. That's life.

With all the holes in that philosophy is it any wonder, I kept looking for something more? I turned to books.

So, What's the Plan?

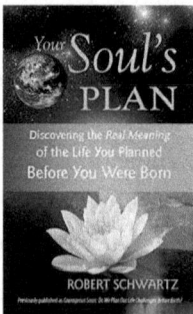

The most informative books I have read on the pre-life and afterlife are *Your Soul's Plan* by Robert Schwartz and the classics of Dr. Michael Newton, *Journey of Souls* and *Destiny of Souls*.

The Newton books came out in the 1990's and began a whole movement of hypnotherapy and past-life regression that is gaining more respectability every year. By revealing a series of case histories, Newton's books give a peek into the afterlife, between lives, and pre-life. Reincarnation is a given. The Newton books, like the studies of Ian Stephenson and Brian Weiss on reincarnation, set the foundation for the ongoing work in this field of exploration.

Schwartz' book, *Your Soul's Plan*, explores pre-life planning. The author became fascinated with the notion that everyone makes a blueprint for their life before each incarnation. Schwartz asked for volunteers on the Internet to investigate their pre-life plan. He interviewed various psychics who tapped into multidimensional information and settled on three he considered the most skilled. Ultimately he focused on ten people for his book. Each represented difficult life challenges--physical illness, addiction, parenting handicapped children, death of a loved one, or accidents. The author engaged three psychics gifted at perceiving pre-life planning sessions to reveal agreements and life lessons for each person.

The book reveals a complicated system. Working with guides, everyone considers the soul growth needed for each incarnation. Members of their soul family work out agreements to play roles in fulfilling their goals. Often these relationships are difficult, even abusive. In other cases, unconditional love will shine through the harshest of circumstances. While there may be karmic balancing involved, it isn't about punishment. Even the worst circumstance imaginable--extreme poverty, illness, or mental cruelty is supposed to be viewed as an opportunity to learn something, at the very least, simple compassion. The bottom line--everyone is responsible for their own life.

The notion of pre-life planning puts a completely new spin on how life works. Imagine that you actually picked your parents. It wasn't random. Don't blame God or bad luck if they were less than ideal. Working with your guides and spirit family group, you came up with a game plan of relationships and challenges. It may include addiction, illness, cruelty or loss. According to Schwartz' book, the challenges are all about soul growth. The ten people in his book all deal with harrowing experiences and come out with fairly positive attitudes. They can see how AIDS or paralysis or losing a child made them stronger, more compassionate people. Finding out it was all part of The Plan, takes self pity out of the equation.

In theory that sounds good. It makes esoteric sense. However, we all know people who didn't rise to life challenges. All I have to do is look at the sad outcomes of several of my relatives and see they were crushed by their life scenarios. When I see a drug addicted homeless man passed out on the beach I think, *Was that The Plan?*

Still, though I sense there's more to the story than captured in Schwartz' book, the concept of pre-life planning resonates with me, along with the notion of Akashic history. Every child comes fully loaded, so to speak. The skills, spiritual insights, weaknesses, and strengths of perhaps hundreds of lifetimes is carried in the DNA. A pre-life planning session sets up key relationships and probabilities. Souls come into agreements. *You will be my father. You will love me, but also give me a hard time.* Lessons will be learned through the relationship.

Understanding pre-life planning erases the right to moan "poor me." Get over your whining about your mother or dad or society. You signed up for this. What are you going to do about it?

We live in a Free Will Zone. The future is not set in stone. The outcome of tomorrow is influenced by the decisions of today. There are probability paths. I enjoy fascinating conversations with Lois Wetzel, an amazing seer. Her books on Akashic Records are featured in that portion of this book.

She told me, "I know I made the right choice when I divorced my husband. I've been shown that had I stayed in the relationship, I would have developed cancer and I'd be gone by now."

A channeled message from Kryon through Lee Carroll discourages referring to "life contracts," because the idea of a "contract" is too specific and rigid. Think of life more as an improvisation. We're given a character, some circumstances and we make it up from there.

Exit Plan

Since life can be more difficult than anticipated, Exit Points are written into The Plan. I've read that everyone has about 5 potential Exit Points. Some are dramatic and others pass almost without notice. The most comprehensive explanation I've read on Exits Points comes from the website of Canadian mystic Sheryl Pedersen at *Spirit Speaks*. She is the scribe for an entity called Lady of the Sun. Here is the information given:

Most of you plan for exit points when you develop the outline of what you are coming to earth to do and experience. You can choose to leave or choose to stay depending on what is happening in your lives at the time and in the lives of those around you. For a leaving affects many other souls and needs to be carefully planned.

For many people, the exit point represents a time when your karma has been cleared and you have done and learned most of what you came here to do and learn. You have the option of returning to spirit, or staying here and creating a new life for yourself, having let go of the past and being free of karmic debt.

When you reach one of these exit points, you arrange to meet with your soul's support team on the other side to discuss what to do, what is best for the soul at this point and what is best for those around them. Much discussion and planning takes place, but ultimately the individual soul makes a choice.

Some people choose to leave because life has gotten very difficult for them to exist in a physical body. Physical bodies do break down and disease, pain and suffering may be experienced. The soul may get weary of the burden of this suffering and decide to leave the physical and continue their work in the spirit realm.

Some people choose to stay and either continue with the same situation they were in, or make other choices, which happens more frequently. They choose another experience, most often something that involves feeling joy and experiencing abundance – another experience they would like to have while in physical form.

What happens really depends on the situation and what is best for the soul and for those around them, for choosing to exit has an impact on all who support the soul while on earth. Because of this, their higher selves are also included in the decision making, having the opportunity to let the soul know their perspective on their choice to leave or stay. And all of the guides and angels involved are allowed to share their ideas and preferences.

All of this information is taken into consideration when making the final decision, which is the decision of the soul who is at the exit point. The choice that they make is always for the highest good although it may not seem to be at the time when those who are left behind experience loss. But remember that loss can be mourned or the transition can be celebrated. You get to choose.

And I'd like to address that which you call suicide. The point of suicide is also an exit point that is part of the divine plan of a soul. If it is appropriate for the soul to leave the physical, they will. If it is not the best time, they will be sent back to complete the work that they came here to do. As with any exit point, there is much planning that goes into the decision of the soul to stay or leave. There is always a perfection in their choice to leave as most often, being in physical form has become very difficult for the soul.

Just know that from the perspective of spirit, there is no judgement on whatever choice the soul has made. Again, the decision is not made in isolation as a grand meeting of souls takes place and the choice that is made is for the highest good of all. That is just what you do when you plan from the perspective of your soul or what you may call your higher self. You make the best possible choice.

You will all find that many people are facing exit points at this time as the earth goes through its grand time of transition. Many souls have completed their soul contracts, cleared karma and can make the choice of experiencing the transition as a being in physical form or a being in spiritual form. The choice is always for the highest good of all. Know this to be true.

Just know that loss will happen for many as they let go of human beings whom they dearly love. Just know that what you call death is not an ending of life, but a transition from physical form to spiritual form. And, whether you choose to mourn or celebrate this transition is a choice that you make.

Blessings, I love you, LOTS – Lady of the Sun

Final Exit

My husband, David, died in a car accident in February of 2013 at the age of 63. When I received the phone call from his best friend alerting me about the accident, I wasn't really surprised.

We'd both had a sense that his days were short. I noticed at Christmas how he seemed to be tying up loose ends. He personally picked out presents for our children and his nephews. In the past, he'd left those tasks to me. He finished his tax information by December 31. We shared some soul-searching conversations.

I thought, *Does he realize he seems to be preparing for death?*

The week before the accident he hand delivered his life insurance premium that guaranteed my financial welfare, bless him.

The last thing he did was slip a Valentine card in the mail to me before heading down the freeway to get to the hospital where his mother was having major surgery. Badly marked road construction set up a confusing scenario that resulted in his death.

Though he didn't know the time or place, I'm certain at some intuitive level he sensed his last Exit Point was imminent. Did it have to be that particular day? I don't know. But an opportunity presented itself and he was gone.

I later had a reading with Helen and she tuned in on the moment of his death. She saw a large white light around him and said an uncle greeted him on the other side. She also saw three previous Exit Points-- one as a small child, one in college, and one in his 30's. I recalled my mother-in-law telling me how sick he was at two with the measles. He wanted her to hold him constantly. Helen thought the college age event was probably a near-miss with a car. At the age of 36, David experienced a major heart attack while we were on vacation in Colorado. At that point in his life, he wasn't very happy. The heart attack didn't come as a surprise to me, despite his young age.

Interestingly, Helen commented, "He could have departed then, but he knew you needed him. He stuck it out for his family."

I've never asked about my Exit Points, but I'm sure I had one in 2003. In fact, it might have been one for all of us -- Paula, Wayne (her husband), Sue and me. At that time, I was taking care of my father in California after he had suffered a stroke. I terribly missed my family and my life in Oklahoma. Sue orchestrated a Sunday afternoon lunch to get me out of the doldrums. Wayne sat in the driver's seat as we sped down the Newport Freeway. From the corner of our eyes, we noticed a vehicle switching lanes towards us very quickly. In the next moment, we realized a U-haul trailer had broken loose from someone's truck and was speeding across the road, uncontrolled. Using his quick reflexes, Wayne gunned the motor and swerved into another lane. The wild trailer barely missed our rear bumper and crashed into the concrete divider. It spun around and cut into traffic again, hitting cars and causing a chain reaction of devastation. We escaped calamity by mere inches and seconds.

That near miss of a car wreck was a wakeup call for me. It put an end to the pity party I'd been throwing myself over the current circumstances. While playing the good daughter, resentment simmered under the surface. My misery was all in my attitude. Looking back, being Dad's reluctant caregiver was definitely part of The Plan. It was so hard, but I learned so much. By the time Dad passed, four years after the stroke, I'd come to a place of peace and gratitude for the journey we had shared together.

Too many people feel like victims of circumstance. Studying pre-life planning is very empowering. Rather than being a victim, be an overcomer. View The Plan with emotional detachment and creativity. If you don't like the current path, change course. There are many possibilities and probabilities. Life is truly what you make it.

Chapter Nine ~ Word Power

Supernal Journals ~ March 31, 2011

Paula, Sue, and I had a prayer session here. The meditation time felt very strong and peaceful, as if we created a spiral of energy in the room. Sue received the phrase, "The hour of decision is upon you." At this time in history we're waging war in Libya. Japan was struck by a terrible earthquake and tsunami that damaged a nuclear power plant.

We specifically sent healing energy to Japan. Paula zoned out for a while. When she came back, she said she'd seen so much energy from all over the world going to Japan. Our prayers joined with others to help mitigate the situation.

Stick and Stones

"Sticks and stones may break my bones, but words will never hurt me." Wrong. That old saying is simply not true. Words have power. They can be destructive, carrying hate and fear. Cyber bullying is mere words, but teenagers are committing suicide over them. Terrorists are recruiting vulnerable followers to leave their families, countries, and friends to join the Jihad. Tweets go viral. 140 characters strung together can ricochet around the world. They can start revolutions, as we saw in the "Arab Spring."

Books are banned because of the power of their words. Bonfires of Bibles have lit up the sky. Missionaries smuggle them into anti-Christian countries, knowing the power of Scripture can change lives and culture. One of the most fascinating books I've read is *The Heavenly Man: The Remarkable Story of The Chinese Christian Brother Yun.* One precious, smuggled underground Bible inspired Brother Yun to share the Christian message, despite cruel imprisonment and decades of government persecution. He memorized the entire Bible and employed those words to begin an underground church movement that has spread like wildfire throughout Asia.

Understanding the power of words is very important. As Stephen King says, they are a form of mental telepathy, transferring ideas and pictures from one mind to another.

Jesus knew the spiritual power of words as he revealed in Matthew 8:18 *Truly I say to you, whatever you bind on earth shall have been bound in heaven; and whatever you loose on earth shall have been loosed in heaven.* KJV

Jesus was a multidimensional thinker!

Learning how to unleash the power of words for positive outcomes is what prayer is all about.

What is Prayer?

Nowadays the word "prayer" carries a lot of baggage. For some people it is a positive expression of faith. For others, it represents hypocrisy or fanaticism.

It's an easy word to toss around. *I'll pray for you....Keep me in your prayers.....*

Let me attempt to define what I mean by "prayer." First, let me state what it is not. Effective praying is not begging. *Please, God, heal my daughter...Please, God, give me this job.* Admittedly, sometimes a last resort prayer of simply, *Please God, help!* can open the door for intervention. Prayers like that often come from people who never think about the Divine until disaster strikes.

The kind of prayer I'm talking about is a daily habit and discipline, like brushing your teeth and taking a shower. It is spiritual hygiene.

Verb or Noun?

Prayer can be a verb. It is an action. Prayers make things happen. They slip into dimensions of reality beyond 3-D and ride into the regions of nonlocal. Distance healing prayer taps into information and transmits healing frequencies.

For example, recently a friend of mine, Mary, asked me to pray for her little dog, Lucy. A tumor needed to be removed from Lucy's leg. The situation brought back a fearful time for Mary. A dog she had loved as a child also had a leg tumor that proved to be malignant. The dog's death remained a painful memory for Mary. Lucy's situation awakened Mary's sleeping, sad memories.

I settled into my prayer chair, opened up my chakras, and pictured Lucy. The site of her tumor appeared in my mind's eye. It looked round and yellow, but not infected. Probably a self-contained fatty tumor. I was glad it didn't look dark and spidery. I pictured the vet's hands in latex gloves performing the surgery, saw the wound healing well.

The images came to me like a little movie. I directed healing energy onto the leg. That was my part of the procedure. The vet was going to do his part. I also sent Mary and her husband some calming energy.

Distance healing prayer is an act of co-creation. It certainly isn't begging. The old paradigm of "turning everything over to God" lacks empowerment. Looking from a Biblical perspective, God created the earth and then gave humans dominion over the earth. God didn't step away. Creation is going on all around us. We're made in God's image--also creators. Prayer is an activity of creation. Healing and manifestation begin with the frequencies of prayer.

Prayer as a Noun

Prayer can be a noun, a group of words expressing holy thoughts. There's *The Lord's Prayer, the St. Francis of Assisi Prayer, The Serenity Prayer*--the list goes on and on. The words of a prayer come together to form a certain energetic frequency. Helen once asked me if I'd ever watched my aura expand by saying The Lord's Prayer. Unfortunately, seeing my aura is a hit-and-miss proposition, but I can feel it.

For centuries Christian congregations have recited traditional prayers in services and masses, creating holy space, whether they recognized the empowerment or not. Certainly, intention plays a big role in truly energizing the power of the words. Saying a prayer from the heart rather than just the lips is like the difference between a professional athlete throwing a baseball and a t-ball pitch, same game but vastly different force.

Positive Thinkers

Scriptures and esoteric material are filled with Words of Divine Guidance. God has been dictating to and through humans since time began. What did Moses bring down from Mt. Sinai after his encounter with God? *Words*--The Ten Commandments. The tablets were so powerful, they were placed in the Ark of the Covenant, known for killing people with its energetic charge.

Nowadays, words are tumbling out of the ether from Ascended Masters, Angels, Nonphysical souls, aliens--via channeling. It's quite a party. One of the most enduring works is *The "I AM" Discourses* from St. Germain. In 1932 a spiritual adventurer named Guy Ballard traveled to Mt. Shasta in California. There, he encountered a man who identified himself as St. Germain. Ballard recorded the Discourses, that read like weekly sermons. Ballard and his wife, Edna, organized and published them under the author name Godfre Ray King, as they are still published today. The Ballards gathered followers that numbered in the thousands for a time. They founded the St. Germain Foundation, which continues its work to this day. The discourses lay down principles that foretell the New Age, with a strong Christian slant. Though the language feels archaic, a world view that includes energy fields, reincarnation (embodiment), and many multi-dimensions are all there for the careful reader to explore.

The first discourse given on October 3, 1932, delves into the power of words.

When you say and feel "I AM," you release the spring of Eternal, Everlasting life to flow on its way unmolested. In other words, you open wide the door to Its natural flow. When you say "I AM not" you shut the door in the face of this Mighty Energy.

"I AM" is the Full Activity of God....

The student, endeavoring to understand and apply these mighty, yet simple Laws, must stand guard more strictly over his thought and expression...For every time you say "I AM not," "I cannot," "I have not," you are, whether knowingly or unknowingly, throttling the "Great Presence" within you.

The whole first discourse continues to reveal the consequences of negative thinking and benefits of positive words, a precursor to Law of Attraction information that took the planet by storm at the end of the 20th century.

Normal Vincent Peale's mid-20th century ground breaking book, *The Power of Positive Thinking,* introduced positive affirmations as life-altering tools. Dr. Peale was an esteemed Christian minister, public speaker, and the founder of Guideposts magazine. I heard once that an original title for the book was *The Power of Positive Prayer*, but was deemed too religious. He passed away in 1993 at the age of 95. Peale ushered in an era of American optimism. Though he had his detractors during his lifetime, the legacy of Peale is still going strong through the continued success of *Guideposts* and their message of inspiration, faith, and hope.

Louise Hay

Positive affirmations have been adopted by success coaches, modern gurus, and influential thinkers of the past seventy years. Louise Hay picked up the affirmation baton from Peale and Ernest Holmes, founder of the Church of Religious Science. Having endured many of life's worst experiences--abuse, rape, unwanted pregnancy, marital betrayal, and cancer--Hay used the positive power of affirmations to heal herself--physically, emotionally, and spiritually. In the mid-1980's she wrote *How to Heal Your Life* and began workshops primarily for gay men caught in the crossfire of the AIDS epidemic. When she couldn't find a publisher for her book, she founded Hay House Publishing. A guest appearance on *Oprah* and a blossoming friendship with Ms. Winfrey catapulted her into the national spotlight.

Hay House Publishing has been the publishing home for many of the leaders of the self-help/spirituality industry of the last forty years, including Wayne Dyer, Deepak Chopra, Abraham/Esther Hicks and more. While most of these folks would shy away from the word "prayer," they understand the link words have to either positive or negative thinking. From the Hay House website:

An affirmation is a positive statement you say or think about yourself. Saying daily affirmations helps reprogram our negative self-talk so we can manifest more positive thinking, feeling and experiences in our lives.

Affirmations employ words to empower and change thinking patterns that ultimately change behavior patterns. That, in turn, radiates out to triggering a change in the Law of Attraction. Our words create our realities. Always saying, "I can't afford that" is like building the walls of financial prison, one word at a time. Adopting affirming phrases like "everything I need flows easily to me," creates an energetic river of abundance.

The Akashic Record Prayer

Some words have been given to us to open portals to multi-dimensions. One of the most interesting stories of a modern prayer is the tale of Johnny Prochaska and his encounter with a

Mayan woman when he received the prayer used to open Akashic Records. The story is related in the book *The Akashic Records* by Ernesto Ortiz and can also be found on the web and through Akashic Records Consultants International (ARCI).

The story began with a man named Johnny Prochaska, a Spanish nobleman of Czechoslovakian lineage, who married into the royal Spanish family. He moved with his family into the Spanish Quarters of Mexico City when civil strife brought Franco to power in Spain.

One day Johnny was to travel for business, but his plane was delayed, so he wandered through the Mexico City barrios to pass the time. As he rounded a crowded street corner, he had an unexpected encounter. A strikingly familiar woman stood in a doorway before him, beckoning him to come. Her face was that of an ancient Mayan woman, and she was one who had called to him in his dreams over the course of three years. As Johnny entered her doorway, she exclaimed, "So! At last you come!"

She told him of the Old Ones, who brought the "knowledge of time" that we now refer to as the Akashic Records; they had brought this sacred information to the earth from far away. The woman guided Johnny on a journey to an ancient sacred site in the mountains, and there he made a deliberate choice to bring the knowledge of the Akashic Records to humanity. Through ceremony, he was given knowledge of the sacred prayer. He was to teach the use of this prayer, which would open the Records to humankind and reawaken all who sought the knowledge. Johnny translated the sacred prayer into Spanish and then English.

The translation I have seen is:

Opening Akashic Records Prayer
I ask God that He will have his shield of Love and Truth around (name) permanently, so only God's Love and Truth will exist between you and me.

I allow the Masters, Teachers, and Loved Ones of (name) to channel through me, out of whatever realm, to say whatever they wish.

Closing Akashic Records Prayer

I thank the Masters, Teachers, and Loved Ones for the information they have given me today. I trust that this information has been given for my highest good. Amen.

Insights and analysis from the *Akashic Records Training* website illuminate the power of the prayer:

This prayer has been taught for 25 years since Johnny Prochaska originally educated Mary Parker about accessing the Akashic Records in his class. What appears to be a simple God-centered prayer in English vibrationally supports a very deep, sensitive internal perspective. The prayer opens the ability to access and hold the connection to the Akashic Records. From this profound vantage point, we assist others and ourselves in answering questions from the level of the soul. This level is filled with light, compassion and understanding. Through questions, specific focus is revealed in the vast Akashic Field. The questions answered are the ones that are truly heartfelt and real, dealing with in-depth development. The actual answers and questions are not linear, but deal with quality of life and underlying influences.

The prayer has five remarkable and distinctive levels of alignment. In summary, it calls forward a shield of protection which is love and truth, it fully attunes to the great consciousnesses who protect and are part of the Akashic Record field of energy, it allows the levels of consciousness to align with the process, and it activates the neutral observer who brings the inner teacher into focus.

The simplicity of the prayer holds power and moves the consciousness well beyond the thinking of everyday life. It offers assistance into deep transcended states and is viewed as sacred. In this state of reverence, we nurture an inner space of stillness through the heart. Remarkably, the

heart energy greatly expands when uninterrupted, and a depth of
wisdom emerges bringing clarity and elucidation to life.

We're entering an era of discovery for the previously disparaged indigenous traditions. The organized destruction of native cultures during Western colonial expansion has eased. A growing appreciation for ancient knowledge is emerging in this age of globalization and satellite communication. Scientists are trekking into the rain forests to learn about healing plants from shaman medicine people. Despite hundreds of years of greed and obliteration, wise men and women have passed on their precious traditions to a few in younger generations, keeping their Light flickering.

My life journey has recently led me to living in Hawaii. I'm discovering a culture that many say goes back to Lemuria, when the ocean was much lower and the islands were one land mass. Native Hawaiians have maintained strong traditions, despite being overpowered by Western forces. Though tensions persist, it is now a blend of East and West, old and new.

A woman living on the island of Oahu named Kahuna Ali'i Wahine Kalei'iliahi traces her ancestral roots down a long line of Royal High Chief Priests and Priestesses. She wears the Priestess mantel and keeps the indigenous beliefs alive. She is a seer and healer. In recent years, she has worked with Lee Carroll/Kryon in seminars and holy ceremonies.

In the book *The Gaia Effect* by Kryon and Monika Muranyi, she offers a prayer that "is traditionally chanted three times. The energy of three acts as a catalyst for change. It is also energy of compassion and the ancients knew this."

Hawaiian Prayer
From the Gods
From the Light
From the Heaven
From the Stillness
From the Heaven
From the Happiness
From the Heaven
From the Life
From the Gods
From the Giver of All Things

I can feel the energetic rhythmic flow from this prayer, even in the English translation. I encourage you to try it as a meditation tool.

Curse Words

A few years ago I planted a Mexican sage plant in my flower bed. I looked forward to enjoying its beautiful, lush purple flowers enhancing the ambiance of my backyard. Alas, it sprouted lots of greenery, but the purple flowers were sparse.

One day I was chatting with a friend about all the backyard plants. I turned to Mexican sage, pointed at it, and said forcefully, "And you! I'm very disappointed in you! You look like a weed." I was just joking around, but I said it with great passion.

The next day I came out to water and discovered the leaves had wilted and turned yellow overnight. The plant went from healthy to dying in a day. Then, I remembered the incident of Jesus and the fig tree.

Mark 11:11-21 NIV

The next day as they were leaving Bethany, Jesus was hungry. Seeing in the distance a fig tree in leaf, he went to find out if it had any fruit on it. When he reached it, he found nothing but leaves, because it was not the season for figs. Then he said to the tree, "May no one ever eat fruit from you again." And his disciples heard him say it....In the morning as they went along, they saw the fig tree withered from the roots. Peter remembered and said to Jesus, "Rabbi, look! The fig tree you cursed has withered!"

I've always felt sorry for that fig tree. We like to believe Jesus never made a mistake and meant to kill that tree as an object lesson on the power of words. But, I wonder if didn't he think, *Oops, sorry*, when he saw the tree, yet turned it into a teachable moment for Peter and the gang.

At any rate, I felt terrible about cursing my poor Mexican sage. I apologized to it as fervently as I'd condemned it. I petted it, channeled healing energy into it, and watered it. Thankfully, it revived and thrived. I enjoyed its purple flowers behind my pool for many seasons until I sold the house. It served as a living object lesson on the power of words, (not to mention plant communication.)

Words have power to curse or to cure. Use them wisely.

The Final Word

The Book of John tells us that Jesus himself was a living prayer. *In the beginning was The Word, and the Word was with God, and the Word was God. He was with God in the beginning. Through him all things were made that has been made. In him was life, and that life was the light of men.*

Words can uplift, create beauty, bring joy, affirm, and spread the Light of God. Follow a Christ-like path and you may become a Living Prayer.

Chapter Ten ~

Manifesting--See it. Feel it. Be it.

Supernal Journals ~ February 25, 2011

Sue had her strongest clairaudient experience yet. She was home alone getting ready for an eye appointment. She "heard" a voice tell her she had visualized many outcomes in her life and brought them into being. She recalled that when Paula was ill and bedridden, in the darkest days of her RSD, Sue consistently visualized Paula wearing shorts and a summer top. A smile lit her face. One day after Paula's healing, Sue drove over to pick her sister up for an outing. Paula walked down the sidewalk smiling, wearing a summer top over shorts. Today Sue recalled the déjà vu moment when her visualization came to fruition. Then she suddenly received a series of images from her life that played like a movie of key moments of her past, showing how she had manifested the outcomes.

She wondered if she could manifest for someone else. She heard, "The stronger visualization will trump the more passive. Let me give you an example. Hitler had a strong vision of Germany as a country without Jews, Blacks, or the handicapped. And for a time that vision came to pass when he drew others into his vision." Sue "saw" scenes of Hitler's Germany.

The voice continued, "But then others in the world perceived Hitler as evil and banded together. They visualized a world without Hitler. Eventually, theirs became the stronger vision and it came to pass."

What is "manifesting?"

The dictionary describes "manifest" as *to make clear or evident to the eye; to show plainly.* In metaphysical lingo it usually means making good things appear in our lives. (Or we shake our heads about how someone we know is *manifesting* bad things.)

The Law of Attraction became all the rage a while back, launched by a series of channeled sessions of a group entity called Abraham through Esther Hicks. (See *Ask and It is Given: Leaning to Manifest Your Desires*) The Cliff Notes version offered in *The Secret* by Rhonda Byrne remains a bestseller. The goal of most people reading these books is to attract wealth and happy relationships into their lives. The principles in these books are valid, if often elusive, as people try to attract worthy lovers and pay off the bills.

Manifesting, making something appear, goes beyond simply becoming rich (though Sue is still working on manifesting a winning lottery ticket). Whether we realize it or not, we are *unconsciously* manifesting the events of our lives, everyday. Through our thoughts and emotional focus, we are creating the unfolding drama of our lives. The goal is to *consciously* create the story of each day.

Think beyond the physical boundaries of the 3-D body into the layers of the auric energetic field. It is there the real connections are made. We are all living magnets, drawing toward us the things we focus upon. If we constantly think about not having enough money, then we are always broke. If we feel nobody likes us, then nobody does. What we project comes back to us.

We attract what we see in our mind's eye. I remember a news story about a woman who installed an elaborate home security system because she was sure she would have a violent home invasion. It happened, despite her precautions. She was a modern-day Job-- *the thing that I have feared has come upon me.*

The first step for positive manifesting is to pinpoint how you are creating frustrating circumstances and begin taking your life take a new direction.   Where is your thinking taking creating problems? Or, as Wayne Dyer would say, where are your "erroneous zones?"

What Would Wayne Do?

In June of 2015 Hay House Publishing sponsored a writer's conference on Maui featuring Dr. Wayne Dyer. Since I had moved to Oahu in February, getting there meant only a puddle jump plane trip, yet I wrestled with spending the money for the event. It seemed frivolous, but spirit-led nagging won out over my penny-pinching persona. I attended the conference.

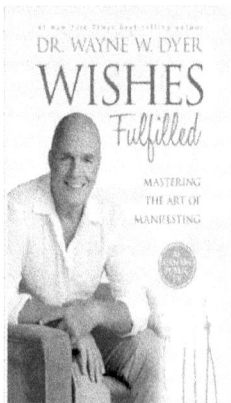

Seeing Wayne Dyer in person was worth every penny. At seventy-five years of age, he exuded a casual, compelling, charisma. Wayne Dyer wasn't pushing his latest book, although he spoke of his books almost like beloved children. He was there to encourage 500 writers to follow their dreams. He told stories about himself--the mistakes made, the chances taken, the lessons learned. Many of Dyer's books illustrate how we create our own realities. His first book, *Your Erroneous Zones: Step By Step Advice for Escaping Your Negative Thoughts and Taking Control of Your Life*, was the number one bestselling book of the 1970's.

His early life had not been easy. After his alcoholic father abandoned the family, his mother was forced to put him and his brothers into the foster care system. He developed a scarcity mentality and a raging bitterness toward his absentee father. Though blessed with a brilliant mind, his deep seated anger and anxieties marred his life. The wisdom in Dyer's books come from first working through his personal challenges. A pivotal day was August 30, 1974, when he stood over his father's grave and found the peace of forgiveness.

He saw the world in a whole new light. He went from focusing on all that he lacked to understanding all he had been given. The errors in his thinking became clear. His early work as a psychologist and counselor revealed the negative power of erroneous thinking, those nasty "erroneous zones." Dyer's brilliance melded through the years with spiritual inspiration to make him one of the most influential persons of his time.

By age 75, Wayne Dyer had become a living manifestation of love and generosity. He often invited strangers he met on Maui into his home for a visit. He purchased homes for 29 people he knew. He recognized the divinity in every person he met. After watching an HBO show about a poor woman in a Southern state who had been incarcerated for a traffic ticket and fines she couldn't pay, he personally paid the $4,000 to get her out of jail.

As it turned out, that June conference was one of his last public appearances. On August 30, 2015, forty-one years to the day after the life-changing experience at the grave of his father, Wayne Dyer passed away in his sleep. He had been full of vitality in June. At the end of August he transitioned through the peaceful, uncomplicated death all of us hope for.

Wayne Dyer left behind a legacy of over forty books and numerous programs to point the way to manifesting abundant, fulfilling living.

What's Your Erroneous Belief?

One of the first steps in manifesting what we want, is to recognize what is blocking our way. As I first delved into my Akash, I asked a question suggested by the Ernesto Ortiz book, *The Akashic Records*.

June 20, 2013 Supernal Journals

What erroneous belief have I held on to?

Answer: "Life is a struggle." Life does not have to be a struggle. Obstacles are illusions you've built to confirm your belief. You've gotten satisfaction when you've overcome these "obstacles."

Erase that notion and simply attract good things and people into your life. No struggles. Surrender to spiritual guidance and all will be easy.

That answer hit me square between the eyes. So true. I had been picturing life as an obstacle course. I often pictured myself as a runner, jumping hurdles set up on a track. Round and round I went, leaping and panting. Exhausting.

For decades I had been projecting my struggles; they materialized; I overcame. I remember worrying about the continuing financial stress, thinking it was some karmic lesson. I'd say out loud, "Haven't I learned the lesson yet?" It took me a long time to realize a poverty mentality help create the struggle.

Since the revelation about obstacle-building, I've consciously switched to thinking--*good things come to me*. I quit running the mental obstacle course. The difference in my life has been profound. The things I need are drawn into my sphere of awareness--into my fields.

A New, Used Car

Positive manifesting includes opening intuitive channels and working with Spirit to get the job done. In 2014, I knew I needed to buy a new car. I HATE buying cars. Too many choices, too little knowledge. In the past, my husband and his car dealer buddy always just delivered the next vehicle. But, after my husband died in 2013, the decisions became mine. I was getting around in my Dad's twenty-year old Lincoln Town Car, a beauty in its day, but now a gas-guzzling boat.

Evaluating the proceeds from life insurance, my financial advisor gave me a price range I could afford, which didn't add up to a new car. I looked online for used cars. I read up on various makes and models, poured through the Sunday ads. Trolled Craigslist. I began to form a picture in my mind of a light colored compact car. Low miles. Heat, air, working windows. No dings. Fuel efficiency. I even imagined someone delivering it to my house and driving away the Lincoln.

Such vehicles appear on Craigslist, but they are snapped up quickly. After a couple of weeks stressing over the listings, I quit the mental torture and decided to just keep driving the Lincoln and calm down. Then, Sue and Paula came over to my house for a Supernal Session. I asked that we request guidance for a new car.

We went into our meditation. Soon, Paula said, "A male relative of yours is here. I see him playing on the ground with you when you were a baby. He had something to do with cars."

"My grandfather? He worked on cars all his life. He died when I was nine. That's fifty years ago."

Paula waved her hand. "He says that's nothing."

For a half-century, I have kept a bear piggy bank that my Grandpa gave me. It has traveled across the country and back again. I knew exactly where it was. I pulled it out of the closet and handed it to Paula. "Here, can you feel him in this?" (Psychometry)

"Oh my gosh," she said, cradling the little bear in her hand, "I feel the waves of love. He is so happy that you have kept something from him. He says he will look for the right car for you. A good fit."

That was enough for me. I stopped driving myself nuts looking at used cars online. The following Saturday evening while watching television I "heard," *go look at Craigslist now.*

I zeroed in on a low mileage silver Nissan Maxima for sale located about ten miles from my house. First thing Sunday morning, I called the number, half-expecting the car to be sold already. But, as "luck" would have it, the owner, a sixty-something Iraqi named Massoud, had been out of town all week. Sue and I met him in a shopping center to give the car a test drive. Massoud was a friendly fellow and by the time the drive was over, we had closed the deal, $1,000 less than my budget allowed. Plus, he was interested in "Daddy's" car. He delivered the Nissan to my house the next morning and, after I fed him a little breakfast and listened to his life story, he drove off with the Lincoln. Wow, I had manifested my visualization-- with a little help from Grandpa, I guess.

Most Benevolent Outcomes

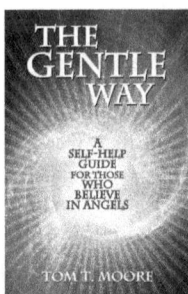 Tom T. Moore offers the concept of asking for Most Benevolent Outcomes in his book *The Gentle Way: A Self-Help Guide for Those Who Believe in Angels.* Moore proposes that we all have a guardian angel hanging around waiting for an invitation to help us in everyday pursuits. He suggests requesting a Most Benevolent Outcome phrased out loud. For example: *I ask for a Most Benevolent Outcome for traveling across town. Please open traffic and keep me safe.* Or *I ask for a Most Benevolent Outcome for finding the perfect dress to wear to the wedding.*

His theory is that by making a verbal request, we have authorized the angelic realm to intercede on our behalf.

The Abraham/Hicks material talks about "segment intending," to visualize positive outcomes for each task of the day. While Moore includes calling on angels, the principle of conscious manifesting is the basic idea.

The exercise of asking out loud for a Most Benevolent Outcome is an easy habit to develop. Part of my morning meditation is to visualize the events before me and ask for a Most Benevolent Outcome for each one. Whether angels are involved, I'm not sure, but the intention is set out clearly and positively. The ripples are sent out. The fields are open. All systems go. Another day has begun.

See it. Feel it. Be it.

As the saying goes, *Change your thinking; change your life.* You want to transform your circumstances? Examine your mental images. How do you see yourself and your circumstances? Don't like the picture? Change it.

See it

Spend time in meditation. Open yourself to higher energies and guidance. Ask for help. Establish a daily quiet time and open your auric fields to connect with a Loving Presence. Name it what you will--God, Source, Higher Self, Jesus, Angels. Be quiet, start to see and hear. Keep a journal of the thoughts and images that pass by. Ask for a new mental picture.

If you want physical changes, visualize a new, improved you. If you want a new career, home, relationship--let the images form. They may seem cloudy at first. Give it time and practice. You may be very surprised by what pops up.

Co-create with Spirit what you need and desire. Visualization is the first step of manifestation.

Feel it

Give the images the power of emotion. How would it *feel* to be that new you? What would it *feel* like to live somewhere else or be in a new relationship? The more emotion you pour into your imagery, the greater the attraction. At the quantum level, you will be drawing what you are seeing into your magnetic fields.

Emotion tied to intention is the engine of manifestation. Become mindful of what your emotions are doing, for they will be projecting what comes your way--either positively or negatively. Design positive outcomes.

Be It

Have the courage to follow your intuition. Ideas will materialize to take you in new directions. Manifesting sometimes requires stepping out of your routines or comfort zones. Act as if the thing you want is already in place or on its way. Going back to getting my car, after the session with Paula and Sue, I believed the right vehicle for me would soon present itself. My frustration dissolved and I eagerly anticipated an answer from Spirit. Live in eager anticipation of positive manifestations.

Movin' On

In February of 2014 I had a talk with myself:

So, Dana, what do you want to do with the rest of your life? You've joined the Widow's Club now. You can stay here in Southern California and hang onto this old house. It's paid for. You're right in the middle between St. Louis and Hawaii where your daughters live. You can visit them twice a year, maybe. You've got some good friends here. The symphony and Friends of the Library will keep you involved with the community. You can write. Is that how you want to ride out your time on planet Earth?

Projecting twenty years down the road, I saw an old lady struggling to keep up an aging property, until the kids finally showed up to move her into an assisted living facility. Hanging onto that "safe" life seemed boring and colorless.

I began to envision a new scenario. Being a part of the grandkids' daily lives. Traveling. Free from house upkeep worries. Meeting new people from different cultures. Writing. Financial freedom. Embracing the unknown.

Selling the family home went from being inconceivable to top priority. I embarked on a new road, one step at a time. Each morning began with meditations and daily instructions. Some days it was as basic as sensing which closet to clean. I asked for help. *Send me a good realtor.... I need a great handyman.* In no time at all, competent professionals came my way.

Manifesting major change is an accumulation of minor daily manifestations. Selling a house is a big deal. You need all the heavenly help you can get. When it was finally time to hold the open houses and take in the offers, I visualized a young couple starting their family and enjoying the house. It took a few weeks for the right people to materialize, but I knew them when I met them.

One thing that bothered me was anticipating dumping all of parents' best items and leaving the house empty for the new occupants. Instead, I pictured walking out of the house with it clean and still furnished, ready for a new family. Leaving it that way made the parting much easier.

As "luck" would have it, that's the way it turned out. I flew off to Missouri before the final closing. The new owners kept some of the pieces and my wonderful realtor disposed of the rest. I didn't have to go through the pain of seeing the house completely gutted.

For me, that was a very kind manifestation from Spirit. It alleviated grief disposing of the favorite furnishings from my parents' happiest days in their home.

In the following months, I set up set up a bedroom and office in my daughter's house in Missouri. My grandkids' voices and laughter echoed through the rooms. The holidays were filled with fun.

After the first of the year in 2015, I bought a one-way ticket to Hawaii. Daughter #2 lives there with her husband and baby. I arrived with no idea where I would be living. In my meditations, I'd seen a house and sidewalk lined with flowering plants.

Affordable housing is scarce, especially in the area surrounding the University of Hawaii. But, as "luck" would have it, within twenty-four hours I secured a wonderful apartment in an old mansion, a short walking distance from my daughter.

This chapter is being written from my perch above a tropical flower-filled courtyard, the sea breeze drifting in through the open window in my apartment. I enjoy walking along the Hawaiian shore. In the distance, whale spouts spray over the turquoise waves. Gorgeous. Exhilarating.

Life is lived one day at a time. I'm enjoying the life I'm manifesting right now very much.

Change The World

Remember Sue's epiphany on manifestation and the Hitler example? Hitler's vision of an Aryan-only society took hold for a while in Germany. The masses united in his vision, gave it power and manifestation, until a more powerful vision pushed back. Sadly, it manifested a world war.

A more positive example would be the *I Have A Dream* speech of Dr. Martin Luther King. A powerful oration on the steps of the Lincoln Memorial began a whole new way of thinking about social equality. New definitions of right and wrong. He shattered the status quo. Dr. King began a massive transformation of the nation's consciousness. His vision is still rippling across the collective consciousness, effecting change. Though it feels slow in coming, Dr. King gave us a new vision to pursue on a national level.

June 23, 2013 ~ Supernal Journals

What is my life purpose?

To bring light and joy into the earth frequency. To raise the frequency to truly fulfill the phrase from the Lord's Prayer "on earth as it is in heaven."

This will happen in increments through mass consciousness. The social media is accelerating the change in mass consciousness frequency levels. There is currently a great deal of chaos as people are beginning to think for themselves and break the mental bondage of religions, government, and dictators.

This is an era when many are identifying as Lightworkers. We sense a call to unite our energy to manifest positive change on the planet. Quantum physicists are proving the power of intention. In the olden days, we called it the power of prayer.

Whatever label you want to give it, there are groups springing up across the globe uniting first in thought and philosophy and then in manifestation. At its worst, we see the terrorist leaders, the New Hitlers, sending out their strong intentions and drawing followers into their legacy of death and destruction.

At its best, there are visionary leaders seeking to bring about a peaceful, equitable, unpolluted world like the Dalai Lama, James Redfield (*The Celestine Vision)*, Todd Jenkins, *Mystery Schools International,* Lee Carroll (Kryon.com), Louise Hay (Hay House Publishing), and Deepak Chopra, to name a few. Oprah Winfrey's OWN network offers Super Soul Sunday. And Pope Francis is really shaking the establishment up at the Vatican.

All of these leaders understand the power of mass consciousness through intention and visualization. They are all trying to persuade us to follow their lead. What's exhilarating about the age we live in, is that we can *think for ourselves.* Even the most restricted societies are seeing the ideological walls cracking and falling.

Now it's up to us to create the world we want for our children and the generations to come. A beautiful, healthy, equitable Planet Earth.

Let us See It...Feel It...Be It.

Epilogue ~

The Supernal Adventure Continues

January 2016

I glance at the clock in my kitschy efficiency Hawaiian apartment in the Manoa Valley, only two miles inland from Waikiki, yet a world away from tourists. Tropical trade winds cool the air. Swishing leaves and coos of zebra doves provide background music as I set up my laptop for a Skype appointment with Kahuna Kaleiiliahi.

As a frequent member of the Kryon team, she conducts blessing ceremonies around the world, seeding new energies in old energy regions. I wonder what the Jewish participants thought of a Hawaiian priestess going to the Holy Land and offering prayers. Pictures and interviews reveal a down-to-earth person, despite supposed high spiritual connection to The Ancients. Her newsletters offer "Talk-Story" themes, so very Hawaiian. We're Facebook friends now.

She claims a lineage of Hawaiian priests and priestesses that harken back to Lemuria. History, as told by Kryon, places the beginning of civilization the land of Lemuria, before it mostly sank into the ocean, leaving only the mountain tops known today as the Hawaiian Islands. The spiritual secrets of the Kahunas have passed down thousands of years, kept alive by the faithful like Kahuna Kaleiiliahi.

I wrestled with the idea of spending money for a counseling session from her. Yet, getting to spend an hour with such a fascinating person seemed like the ideal Christmas present for a spiritual adventurer such as myself. Now through the modern magic of Skype, I could visit with the Kahuna in the comfort of my little home. Her email explained she could tap into information from my spiritual team through her sacred team.

As I settle in my chair, pulling up the Internet, I don't have a list of questions. Mainly, I'm curious about her. I've been around enough seers to know the beings on the Otherside are already familiar with my issues.

I think back to that first session with Joanne the Akashic Records reader back in 2005 and how nervous I was. My knees actually shook as I stepped into her office, wrapped in a cloak of Bible Belt fear. Now, a decade later, I shimmer with quiet anticipation at my session with a Hawaiian priestess. Fearless.

The computer bubbles and the Skype screen comes alive. The Kahuna Kaleiiliahi is calling. We say hello and marvel at modern technology. She is at her home on the Big Island. I sit on Oahu.

I give her a brief history of my life, a marriage of 34 years, two daughters, the passing of my husband three years ago. I tell her of his conservative Christian perspective and how he would have been appalled at me consulting mediums and seers. And how amusing I've found it that at every opportunity since he's passed, he has shown up at any session I attended with a capable medium in the room.

She smiles and says, "He's here now."

I laugh. "Of course he is."

"He's saying he left partly as a gift to you. He was finished with his life mission and he would have held you back. This is your time now. You need to get ready. Your husband is part of your planning team."

I've been aware that my husband's death provided me with the freedom to make life decisions without putting him into the equation.

Though I've certainly missed him and our life together, I'm also exploring avenues that would have been impossible as his wife.

Then she says, "I don't usually tell people about myself because they are paying to get information about themselves, but I am being directed to tell you some of my story."

Of course, "they" know learning more of her story will satisfy my curiosity. Kaleiiliahi also entered a new era of life when her husband passed away over a decade ago. Spiritual teachers appeared, including Kryon and Kahuna Holi Makua. After years on the mainland, she returned to Hawaii to assume the spiritual leader mantle and bring a feminine energy to the station of Kahuna. In her younger days, she could have never imagined traveling all over the globe, meeting spiritual leaders, offering ceremonies and prayers for higher energies. That is the life she lives today and still expresses amazement at what is unfolding.

Returning to the information directed for me, she tells me, "Get ready. It's time. Your way of fulfilling your mission is through writing. Your next book will be 100% channeled. You'll have a lot of help."

I balk at that. One hundred percent channeled? Seriously? I don't think I have the psychic wiring for that. I express my doubts, "I'm like a Model T brain when you need a new Tesla for that kind of work."

She laughs and says, "I totally dismiss that nonsense. You have done this before. You need to search in your Akash and find it. You are like many old souls who have the seed fear of Enlightenment. You have lived time after time where you were beaten down, even killed when you expressed your gifts. That was the old energy. But now, look around, we're seeing an explosion of people offering their healing gifts, spiritual teachings, channeling Ascended Masters. They are all over the Internet, giving lectures, and writing books. And nothing bad is happening to them. They are working in freedom. It's part of the new energy. But, many still remember the lives of persecution. Write this down. I have a prayer for you to repeat until you don't need it anymore. It's Releasing the Seed Fear of Enlightenment.

Place your hand over your heart and say this three times every evening before you go to sleep.

Dear body, in all sacredness and love I speak to you. FEAR NOT! It is finally safe for us to come out of the cave and use our mastery to serve humanity. LET'S DO IT!"

She says, "Now is the time for you to step away from the Mother role. You have other avenues of your soul to explore. Your daughters will look back and thank you for showing them you could develop aspects beyond mothering. Women have been conditioned to believe being the mother and grandmother is their main value as a human being. You will see there is more to your life mission."

She gives me another affirmation to write out and see on a daily basis:

Of all my lifetimes, this is my grandest. This is the one I've been waiting for. I'm ready for it. And I claim it.

I express my trepidation at being alone. She nods knowingly, "Everyone fears being alone, but you are not alone. You have your whole team with you leading the way. You will be meeting people on the path who will compliment the work you're doing. Write this down: *not only am I never alone, but I draw to myself all the people and situations to enhance my life.*"

Our hour comes to an end. The Kahuna says our meeting was a divine appointment. I thank her for our session. The call disconnects.

She's given me much to think about. Most of what she said confirms thoughts that have floated through my mind. Yet, hearing someone tell you to sally forth and live your life with fearless intent is inspiring. She said 2016 = 9 in numerology, a year of completion. I smile. Guess I should finally complete this manuscript.

The future is what we make it, what we envision and call into our physical reality. We do that individually and corporately as human beings unfolding our history. Now is the time for us to choose a better future for every person and the whole planet. It begins with conscious intention. Choose love over fear, freedom of thought over mental incarceration.

Let the inherited hatreds, bigotries, feuds and grudges go. That's all part of the Old Energy. Step into the New Energy. Embrace beauty, peace, balance, and fairness. Forgive.

Embark on Supernal Adventures. I'll see you there!

About the Author

Raised in the cultural crossroads of Southern California, Dana Taylor explores spirituality, healing, relationships, and multidimensional living in her writing. Her search for personal wellness lead to studying alternative medicine, essential oils, and energy healing. She is a Reiki Master. Her books have won various awards including Golden Quill Awards Best First Book (*Ain't Love Grand*), and 2014 Independent Spirit Book Awards - Energy Medicine Category (*Ever-Flowing Streams: Christ, Reiki, Reincarnation & Me)*. She has frequently been on the Amazon Bestseller lists. Currently, she divides her time between Hawaii, Missouri, and California. Find her on the web SupernalLiving.com and DanaTaylorAuthor.com.

A note from Dana: If you enjoyed this book, please take a moment to write a brief Amazon review and perhaps give it a shout-out on the social media. Thank you!

The Supernal Friends

Paula

Sue

Helen

www.ingramcontent.com/pod-product-compliance
Lightning Source LLC
Chambersburg PA
CBHW061730020426

42331CB00006B/1179